Simply . . . Gluten-free
Quick Meals

ALSO BY CAROL KICINSKI

Simply . . . Gluten-free Desserts:
150 Delicious Recipes for Cupcakes, Cookies, Pies,
and More Old and New Favorites

More Than 100 Great-Tasting

Recipes for Good Food Fast

ᕦᕤᕦᕤᕦᕤ

Simply . . . Gluten-free
Quick Meals

Carol Kicinski

THOMAS DUNNE BOOKS
St. Martin's Press
New York

THOMAS DUNNE BOOKS.
An imprint of St. Martin's Press.

SIMPLY . . . GLUTEN-FREE QUICK MEALS. Copyright © 2012 by Carol
Kicinski. All rights reserved. Printed in the United States of America. For
information, address St. Martin's Press, 175 Fifth Avenue, New York, N.Y.
10010.

www.thomasdunnebooks.com
www.stmartins.com

Design by Kathryn Parise

LIBRARY OF CONGRESS CATALOGING-IN-PUBLICATION DATA

Kicinski, Carol.
    Simply — gluten-free quick meals : more than 100 great-tasting
recipes for good food fast / Carol Kicinski.
        p. cm.
    ISBN 978-0-312-62207-7 (hardcover)
    ISBN 978-1-4299-4134-1 (e-book)
    1. Gluten-free diet—Recipes.   2. Quick and easy cooking.
3. Cookbooks.   I. Title.
    RM237.86.K534   2012
    641.5'63—dc23

                                                        2011046509

First Edition: April 2012

10 9 8 7 6 5 4 3 2 1

For my hubby, Thom, my chief taste tester,
biggest supporter, and the love of my life

Contents

Introduction   1

Stocking Your Gluten-Free Pantry   3

Quick-Cooking Strategies   11

Quick Mixes   15

Simple Suppers   31

Easy Entertaining   101

Get Up and Go   159

Pantry Raid   169

Slow, Slow, Quick, Quick   185

Many Thanks   197

Index   199

Simply . . . Gluten-free
Quick Meals

Introduction

ᘒᘒᘒᘒᘒᘒᘒᘒᘒ

Whether you are new to a gluten-free diet and are looking for recipes and menus to get you started, live in the fast lane with little time for cooking, or are just looking to increase your repertoire of go-to gluten-free dishes, this book offers recipes, ideas, and strategies that will make your time in the kitchen, and possibly your life, a little easier.

I love to eat, cook, and entertain. In a perfect world I would possess unlimited time in which I could pursue these endeavors. The sad reality is that I do not live in a perfect world and the demands of work, family, and other obligations consume a huge amount of my time. And I believe I am not alone.

No matter how hectic our daily schedules are, eat we must. And if I must eat, I must eat well. Having a limited amount of time does not mean I want to compromise the quality of what I eat.

Being gluten-free can add to the challenge of preparing quick meals. We do not have the same abundance of convenience foods available to us as the average person. Some may look at this as an inconvenience. However, I see the upside of avoiding the unhealthy chemical additives and highly processed ingredients so often found in prepackaged foods.

It is a terrible thing when a passion starts to feel like drudgery. As much as I love my time spent in the kitchen (with the exception of the cleaning up!) even I can get harried when I have just thirty minutes to feed six people. I never want to resent making a meal as creating and preparing food for people is one of my great passions.

I consider myself somewhat of a lazy person, always looking for time-savers

and shortcuts, but ironically I am also a person who tries to cram as many activities into each day as is humanly possible. Given this dichotomy and the fact that I want any project or meal I undertake to be done to the best of my ability, I have learned and developed tips and strategies over the years for preparing delicious, gluten-free meals quickly and easily.

Whether you love to cook or just do it because you have to, my hope is that this book will spark your imagination, give you some guidelines, and serve as a springboard for your own creativity in the kitchen.

Stocking Your Gluten-Free Pantry

෯෯෯෯෯෯෯෯෯

I have lived my whole life in areas of the world that tend to be unexpectedly hit by natural disasters, such as earthquakes and hurricanes. So I have learned the value of a well-stocked pantry. But of course life has a way of throwing everyday emergencies at you, and it is at times like that when the pantry can be your saving grace.

Whether you have five minutes or five hours to get food on the table, the pantry is the best place to "go shopping." After all, no one wants to run to the store every time they have a meal to prepare.

I consider the freezer, refrigerator, and spice cabinet part of my pantry as well as the actual pantry itself. You might think that as a cookbook writer and recipe developer I would have a huge pantry. Nothing could be further from the truth. Most people have more space in their broom closet than I have in my actual pantry. This being the case, I must choose wisely what I put in it. Here is a list of what I consider the essentials.

Almond Flour. Great for grain-free baking and cooking. Look for finely ground, blanched almond flour. It is available in health food stores and on the Internet. Recently I have started seeing it in regular grocery stores.

Almond Milk. A great dairy-free milk alternative, I use almond milk for baking, adding to cereal, and in desserts. Unopened almond milk containers can be stored in the pantry.

Baking Powder. A leavening agent that helps cakes and breads rise, I use aluminum-free, double-acting baking powder. Corn-free baking powder is also available.

Baking Soda. Used in baking as a leavening agent, it also has a wide variety of other purposes so it earns its place on my pantry shelves.

Brown Rice Flour. I use only superfine as it produces far superior results and is a great way to add whole grains to your gluten-free diet. My favorite brand is Authentic Foods. It is available in natural food stores and on the Internet.

Canned Beans. I love dried beans and always stock them, but unless I have hours to soak and cook them, canned beans are a go-to staple. I stock a variety: black, white, kidney, and chickpeas. They are great for making quick soups, for adding to salads, and for stews and casseroles.

Canned Coconut Milk. Coconut milk is my preferred dairy-free alternative for baking and in making desserts and some sauces. I stock both full fat and low fat. The full-fat milk has a pronounced coconut flavor while in the low-fat version the coconut flavor is much less pronounced.

Canned Fruit. Of course I prefer fresh fruit but I do stock a few cans of my favorite canned fruits such as dark sweet cherries, peaches, pineapple, and mandarin oranges for last-minute desserts and for adding some zing to salads.

Canned Mild Chilies. These not-too-spicy chilies add depth of flavor and a little heat to Latin-inspired dishes.

Canned Tomatoes. Unless tomatoes are in season "fresh" ones can be tasteless. For soups, stews, and sauces I always keep a stock of canned tomatoes on hand. The tomatoes for canning are picked ripe and canned shortly after, often making them a better choice unless it is the peak of tomato season. I stock both small and large cans and love the San Marzano tomatoes from Italy but I will also buy store-brand cans of diced tomatoes when they are on sale.

Canned Tuna. Great for a quick lunch, mixed with some mayonnaise and veggies and wrapped in a lettuce leaf. I keep both tuna packed in water and in olive oil so I can choose depending on my mood and the number on my bathroom scale.

Chipotles in Adobo Sauce. Smoked jalapeño peppers in red sauce can add smoky depth of flavor to dishes as well as heat. They come in small cans and

are sold in the ethnic section of the grocery store. I rarely use a whole can in one recipe so I open the can, pour the contents in the blender, puree, and store in a small jar in the fridge; this way I can use just as much as I need for any given recipe. I add it to mayonnaise or stir it into sauces, stews, and even salad dressings.

Chocolate. I keep bags of good-quality bittersweet and semisweet chocolate chips on hand at all times. Stay away from inexpensive store brands as they often contain wax fillers. In my world, chocolate is an essential.

Condiments. With a good stock of condiments you can whip up a tasty meal with little thought or planning. I am never without ketchup, hot pepper sauce, such as Tabasco, chili garlic paste, gluten-free soy sauce, fish sauce, a variety of mustards, A.1. Steak Sauce, gluten-free taco sauce, Worcestershire sauce, and jarred salsa. Jams and jellies are a must as well. See note above under mayonnaise about cross contamination.

Cornstarch. Good for thickening soups, sauces, and gravies. If you are intolerant to corn, use tapioca starch or arrowroot powder instead.

Dried Fruit. It is great to keep a variety of your favorites on hand not just for snacking but for sprucing up salads, baking, and adding variety to stews. You can typically find cherries, cranberries, apricots, and dates in my pantry. I use dates in baking and cooking as a natural sugar substitute.

Dried Gluten-Free Pasta. After much trial and error I finally found a brand of dried gluten-free pasta I like, Tinkyada. It comes in both white and brown rice varieties and in various shapes. You may find you prefer a different brand but whatever kind you like, it is always a good idea to have a few bags for when you need a quick go-to meal.

Dried Herbs and Spices. I keep a variety of peppers: black, cayenne, and hot red pepper flakes as well as paprika, cumin, sage, bay leaves, thyme, rosemary, oregano, chili powder, coriander, curry powder, Italian seasoning, poultry seasoning, garlic powder, dried onion, ginger, nutmeg (always whole to grate as needed), cinnamon, and cloves. I have a few more odds and ends in there but

these are the ones I reach for on a regular basis. Many people think that spices last forever but they only have a shelf life of six months or so before they lose their flavor. Go through your spice cabinet and replace your dried herbs and spices on a regular basis.

Dried Mushrooms. A little packet of dried mushrooms doesn't take up much space in the pantry but they add amazing depth of flavor in stews and soups.

Extracts. Always buy pure extracts such as vanilla and almond. Not only are imitation extracts inferior in taste, they often contain gluten.

Frozen Vegetables and Fruits. Before you scoff, realize that frozen vegetables and fruits are flash frozen almost immediately after picking, which means they are often fresher than the veggies you have languishing in your refrigerator drawer. Also certain vegetables are just so much more convenient in frozen form. It takes pounds of spinach to produce the same amount in one small frozen package, shelling enough peas or peeling enough baby onions for a family can take ages when fresh but they come already prepared in frozen form. I typically stock frozen peas, corn, spinach, baby onions, raspberries, strawberries, mixed berries, and mango chunks.

Gluten-Free Cake Mixes. As much as I love to bake from scratch, you never know when you might have an emergency cupcake need. With a little doctoring, the new mixes taste almost as great as homemade.

Gluten-Free Chicken and Beef Stock. Now available in most grocery stores, I like the type that comes in a box as it can be stored in the refrigerator without transferring into another container. An essential for making soups, stews, gravies, and sauces.

Gluten-Free, Graham-Style Crumbs and Crackers. These are perfect for making a quick gluten-free crust for pies and cheesecakes. Available in some regular grocery stores, health food stores, and on the Internet.

Gluten-Free, Panko-Style Bread Crumbs. Perfect for breading meat and fish or for adding a crunchy topping to casseroles and such. Made by Kinnikin-

nick, this is one of my favorite gluten-free products. Available in some regular grocery stores, health food stores, and on the Internet.

Gluten-Free Sandwich Bread and English Muffins. I store my gluten-free bread and English muffins in the freezer, so I believe they can be classified as pantry items.

Ice Cream. There is no better quick dessert than ice cream, either full of dairy or dairy-free. I sometimes even melt vanilla ice cream and use it as a sauce for cakes and pies.

Jarred Roasted Red Peppers. It doesn't take long to roast red peppers at home but you have to think ahead and buy the fresh peppers first. The great thing about the canned variety is they sit there waiting for you until the moment when inspiration strikes unexpectedly.

Jarred Tomato Sauce. For those times when I don't have all day to simmer tomato sauce I find jarred a perfectly good replacement—although I do doctor it up with fresh onions and garlic, a can of diced tomatoes, extra herbs, and perhaps a splash of red wine.

Mayonnaise. I keep good-quality mayonnaise and egg-free mayonnaise substitute (such as Vegenaise) on hand for making creamy dressings and for baking. If you have non-gluten-free people in your household, you need to make sure they do not use a knife for spreading mayo on their bread and then stick it back into the mayo (or any other condiment or jam) jar, otherwise cross contamination can occur and you could become ill. If you cannot trust that they won't be extra-cautious, you may want to have your own designated gluten-free jar.

Millet. I keep whole millet on hand for making hearty, whole grain hot cereal. I also use millet flour in baking.

Nonstick Cooking Spray. This is such a time-saver. It is so much easier to spray a pan than it is to brush on oil or butter. Do not buy baker's nonstick cooking spray as it contains flour and thus gluten. Organic varieties are now also available.

Nuts and Seeds. I keep a variety of nuts and seeds on hand. I buy them in bulk, which saves money, and store them in the freezer, which extends their shelf life. Nuts can be ground for making gluten-free, grain-free pie crusts, they are great for coating fish, chicken, and pork, dressing up salads, and they are wonderful for snacking.

Oats. Buy only certified gluten-free oats. Oats themselves do not naturally contain gluten but due to growing and manufacturing processes, cross contamination can be a problem.

Oils. As I said, I don't have a huge pantry so I stock extra-virgin olive oil, grapeseed oil, and sesame oil. I find that in most cases these three will fill any need I have.

Olives. I keep a variety of olives on hand not just for using in recipes but also to use as an emergency appetizer for unexpected guests. I stock kalamata, Spanish green olives, and even small cans of sliced black olives.

Peanut and Sunflower Butters. I keep both on hand for baking and for when I need a quick snack. I stock sunflower butter so I can prepare nut-free dishes.

Potato Starch. Also an ingredient in my Sweet Rice Flour Blend, potato starch is not the same as potato flour. It is available in natural food stores and on the Internet.

Quinoa. The whole grain superfood, this is great for gluten-free porridges, pilafs, and as an alternative to rice or couscous. I buy prerinsed quinoa as it saves precious time in the kitchen.

Rice. I always have arborio and brown rice on hand as well as instant rice for those times when I need a really quick meal.

Salt. I cook exclusively with either kosher or fine sea salt. If you use regular table salt, use half the amount called for in the recipes.

Sweet Rice Flour (also known as glutinous rice flour). I buy either superfine or Asian.

Sweeteners. I always have granulated, raw, brown, and confectioners' sugar

on hand as well as agave nectar, maple syrup, and palm or coconut sugar for when I want unrefined sweeteners.

Tapioca Starch. Available at Asian markets and natural food stores, this is good for thickening sauces and gravies. It is also an ingredient in my Sweet Rice Flour Blend. Asian tapioca starch is less expensive.

Vinegars. I stock a few more varieties of vinegar than oil: balsamic, red, and white wine. Sherry, apple cider, and rice vinegars each fill their own niches. If space was not an issue for me I would probably keep even more varieties but these fill most of my needs. I don't buy bottled salad dressing because it is so easy to make it from scratch so I figure I have earned a little extra pantry space for vinegars.

White Rice Flour. I buy either superfine or Asian white rice flour in bulk and keep it on hand for making gluten-free flour blends. They are available in natural food stores, Asian markets, and on the Internet.

Xanthan or Guar Gum. Used in baked goods and in my Sweet Rice Flour Blend, it helps hold gluten-free baked goods together. Available in natural food stores and on the Internet. I store mine in the freezer. For people with corn allergies, choose guar gum instead of xanthan gum.

Quick-Cooking Strategies

There are a few key elements to getting a meal on the table quickly. One is organization. If you have things where you can find them and put them back in their place, you won't waste time searching for something you need.

Menu planning is another time-saver. Personally, I have never been one to plan out a whole week's menu and then follow that plan. After all, on Sunday I may have planned to have beef on Tuesday, but when Tuesday comes around I may be in the mood for fish. However, having a general idea of what you may want to eat the coming week and shopping accordingly just makes good sense. There are certain fresh items I always have on hand and replace weekly: eggs, cream, Parmesan cheese, butter (unsalted always), onions, garlic, fresh herbs, potatoes, fresh seasonal vegetables, salad fixings, meat, poultry, fish, and fresh seasonal fruit.

While I would be happy to shop every day for food, it is just not practical. Every couple of months it is a good idea to do a big restocking. If possible go to one of those big box stores and buy certain foods in bulk; this saves not only time but also money. Buy fresh foods weekly. With a variety of food on hand you can always figure out something to eat.

A big time-saver during the week is to wash up the fruits and veggies and apportion the proteins if needed before putting them away. Taking a few extra minutes on grocery shopping day saves a huge amount of time during daily meal preparation.

Restaurants have to prepare a lot of meals quickly, so they employ something called *mise en place*. *Mise en place* is a French term that literally means "to

set in place." The chef reviews the menu and gets out everything he or she will need to prepare the menu, then washes and chops the vegetables and fresh herbs and has them ready when it comes time to cook. They get out the pots and pans, spatulas and knives they need, and preheat the ovens. When it is time to cook, they can do so uninterrupted. This is a brilliant strategy to employ at home as well. It is always a good idea to review a recipe fully before starting; nothing is worse than being halfway through making a dish and finding out you don't have an ingredient or the proper equipment. Think through your menu the same way a chef does: for example, if garlic or parsley is called for in two recipes, chop the amount you need for both at the same time.

The next element in creating great meals quickly is to start with great ingredients that do not require a lot of fuss to make them taste great. A bowl of perfectly ripe strawberries can be as good a dessert, if not better, than a complicated torte. Great salad greens need only a simple dressing of lemon juice or vinegar and good olive oil to make them spectacular.

Don't be afraid to take help where you can get it. Nowadays you can buy preprepped vegetables and salad greens that can be huge time-savers. I am also a huge fan of the supermarket rotisserie chicken; it doesn't cost very much more than buying a raw chicken and can be used in a number of ways: shredded for salads, soups, and stews, turned into chicken tacos with the addition of a corn tortilla and some salsa, or just served as is with a squeeze of fresh lemon juice to brighten it up. Some chickens are injected with gluten-containing ingredients so make sure you check with your particular store.

As far as quick-cooking equipment goes, there are a few items I believe to be lifesavers: good-quality, sharp knives, microplane graters, spoons, tongs and spatulas, measuring spoons and cups, whisks, silicone spatulas, strainers, a food processor, a microwave, a mixer, a good blender, sturdy pots and pans that can be used stovetop or in the oven, and a slow cooker. It is better to have a few good-quality pieces of kitchen equipment that are multipurpose than to have cupboards and drawers full of gadgets that have only one purpose.

The oven is one of the greatest labor-saving devices we have and it is often overlooked. People tend not to think of roasting as a method of quick cooking, but the truth is that with minimal preparation you can roast meats, fish, poultry, vegetables, and fruits and reap great rewards. Stir-frying and sautéing can be fast but you need to stand over the stove to do it whereas with roasting the oven does all the work and you get all the credit.

The following chapters contain recipes and strategies to help you get delicious, gluten-free food on the table fast, no matter the occasion or time of day.

Quick Mixes

TAKING A LITTLE TIME to prepare a few basic gluten-free flour blends will help speed you along in cooking and baking. Included in this chapter are a few you can prepare ahead and keep on hand in either the pantry or freezer. Not only is making your own gluten-free flour blend and pancake and biscuit mix less expensive than purchasing ready-made from the store, but also the quality is so much better. My gluten-eating friends are always amazed that the gluten-free baked goods I prepare taste just as good, if not better, than their gluten-filled counterparts. The trick to pulling off this feat is starting with a really good gluten-free flour blend or baking mix.

Sweet Rice Flour Blend

• Dairy-Free

Make 9 cups
flour mix

I am including this recipe from my first book, Simply . . . Gluten-free Desserts, here again because it is a terrific, pastry-quality, all-purpose, gluten-free flour blend. It can be used as a cup-for-cup replacement for regular all-purpose wheat flour. Making your own flour blend at home saves money and ensures you will get terrific results. Spend a couple of minutes mixing up a batch of this sweet rice flour blend and you will have an all-purpose, gluten-free flour on hand when you need it. Store your flour blend in an airtight container in your pantry or in plastic freezer storage bags in the freezer.

All gluten-free flours are not created equal; use superfine or Asian white rice and sweet rice flour, and your final dishes will have no gritty texture or cardboard flavor. Sweet rice flour is also sometimes called glutinous rice flour. Superfine rice flours can be purchased on the Internet or in health food stores. Purchasing Asian rice flours from an Asian market will be less expensive than buying them from the health food store. Tapioca flour is also sold in Asian markets, again at far less cost than from the health food store.

4 1/2 cups superfine white rice flour
1 1/2 cups sweet rice (glutinous) flour
2 cups potato starch (not potato flour)

1 cup tapioca flour (also known as tapioca starch)
4 teaspoons xanthan or guar gum

In a large mixing bowl, slowly whisk all the ingredients together very well, making sure they are evenly distributed.

This recipe can easily be halved, doubled, or tripled.

Basic Pancake and Biscuit Mix

~~~~~~

• Dairy-Free

Makes 6 cups
mix

This is a great basic mix that can be used for making pancakes, biscuits, muffins, shortbread, and quick breads. I realize that you can now purchase premade, gluten-free biscuit mix but making it at home not only saves you money, it also ensures that you can control the quality of the ingredients used; you can decide the amount and type of sugar (or other sweetener) you add, eliminate hydrogenated oils, and make sure that nothing but good-quality ingredients goes into your food.

This recipe starts with the Sweet Rice Flour Blend and will produce light, delicate pancakes and baked goods that are as good if not better than those made with regular wheat flour. This mix is also very versatile.

When you are ready to start cooking, simply add liquid, fat, eggs (or egg substitute), and possibly some type of sugar to the mix for making things such as muffins or pancakes. This gives you lots of flexibility: if you like butter, use that as your fat; for dairy-free you can add grapeseed oil, coconut oil, vegetable oil, nondairy butter substitute, or whatever type of dairy-free fat you prefer. The same goes for the type of liquid you use; you can use any type of milk or dairy-free milk you like, or even fruit juice.

Make up a batch of this mix, store it in an airtight container in the pantry or in a plastic storage bag in the freezer, and you can get pancakes or muffins on the table in no time with very little effort and lots of options.

6 cups Sweet Rice Flour Blend (page 17)	3 teaspoons kosher or fine sea salt
6 teaspoons baking powder	

In a large mixing bowl, slowly whisk all the ingredients together very well, making sure they are evenly distributed.

This recipe can easily be halved, doubled, or tripled.

Basic Pancakes

• Dairy-Free
Adaptable

Makes 12
pancakes

Starting with the Basic Pancake and Biscuit Mix, you have lots of options as to what goes into your pancakes. The liquid can be milk or the dairy-free milk of your choice, the liquid fat can be melted butter or dairy-free butter substitute, any type of oil you prefer such as coconut or grapeseed or even bacon fat, and the sugar can be substituted with the sweetener of your choice. You can also tailor these pancakes to suit your own personal preferences, adding more or less sweetener. Add a little more liquid for thinner pancakes, less if you like your pancakes thicker.

While these basic pancakes are delicate and delicious on their own, they can also be changed up by stirring in a cup of fruit such as blueberries or sliced bananas. Stir the fruit in after the batter has been mixed. For savory pancakes, omit the sugar and vanilla.

1½ cups Basic Pancake and
   Biscuit Mix (page 18)
2 large eggs
1 cup liquid (milk, dairy-free milk,
   etc.)
1 teaspoon pure vanilla extract

¼ cup liquid fat (melted butter,
   bacon grease, grapeseed or
   coconut oil, etc.)
2 tablespoons sugar (or
   equivalent amount of
   another sweetener)

Whisk all the ingredients together in a large mixing bowl until fully combined and smooth. If adding fruit or other flavor agents, add them now.

Heat a skillet or griddle over medium heat until a drop of water sizzles immediately when splashed onto the hot pan. Lightly grease the skillet with gluten-free, nonstick cooking spray, melted butter, or oil. Ladle ¼ cup of batter onto the pan for each pancake. Cook until the top of each pancake is bubbly, the edges appear dry, and the bottom is lightly browned, about 2 minutes. Flip and cook until the opposite side is browned, 1 to 2 minutes. Repeat with the remaining batter. The pancakes can be kept warm in a low (200-degree) oven until serving.

Basic Muffins and Quick Breads

• Dairy-Free
Adaptable

As with the pancake recipe, you have lots of options here. This is a basic muffin and quick bread recipe to which you can add fruit, nuts, and seeds. The liquid can be milk or the dairy-free milk of your choice, and the fat can be melted butter, bacon grease, or whatever oil you prefer.

You can also make savory muffins with this recipe; just omit the sugar and vanilla extract and add any herbs and spices you like such as rosemary, curry powder, or cayenne pepper, chopped sautéed vegetables, diced chilies, grated cheese, corn kernels—you name it. About a cup of mix-ins will work for the whole batch.

1 1/2 cups Basic Pancake and
Biscuit Mix (page 18)
2 large eggs
1 cup liquid (milk, dairy-free milk,
etc.)
1/4 cup liquid fat (melted butter,

bacon grease, grapeseed or
coconut oil, etc.)
1/2 cup sugar (or equivalent
amount of another sweetener)
1 teaspoon pure vanilla extract

Preheat the oven to 350 degrees. Line a 12-cup standard muffin pan with paper baking liners. For quick bread, spray a 9 × 5-inch loaf pan with gluten-free, nonstick cooking spray.

Put the Basic Pancake and Muffin Mix in a large mixing bowl. Break the eggs into another mixing bowl, whisk lightly, add the remaining ingredients, and whisk to combine. Add the wet ingredients to the Basic Pancake and Biscuit Mix and stir to combine; a few lumps are OK. If you want to add fruit or other flavorings, do so after the batter has been mixed. Divide the batter among the prepared muffin cups and bake for 25 to 30 minutes, or until a toothpick inserted into the center of a muffin comes out clean and the muffins are browned.

For a quick bread, pour the batter into the prepared pan and bake for 50 to 60 minutes, or until a toothpick inserted into the center comes out clean and the top is nicely browned. Run a knife around the edges when it comes out of the oven. Let the loaf cool in the pan for 5 minutes, then transfer it to a wire rack to finish cooling.

Makes 12 muffins or one 9 × 5-inch loaf

VARIATIONS

Blueberry: Add 1 cup fresh or thawed frozen blueberries.

Apple Cinnamon: Replace the sugar with brown sugar, add 1 teaspoon ground cinnamon, and 1 cup of diced apples.

Banana Nut: Reduce the liquid to ¾ cup, add 1 cup mashed bananas, and ½ cup chopped nuts.

Cranberry Orange: Use orange juice for the liquid, increase the sugar to ¾ to 1 cup, add the finely grated zest of an orange, ½ teaspoon baking soda, and 1 cup chopped fresh or frozen cranberries.

Chili Cheese: Omit the sugar and vanilla, add 1 small can of diced mild green chilies, and 1 cup of grated sharp cheddar cheese.

Basic Biscuits

• Dairy-Free
Adaptable

• Vegetarian/
Vegan Adaptable

These biscuits can be rolled and cut with a cookie cutter, dropped by spoonfuls and baked for drop biscuits, spooned on top of simmering stew for dumplings, and sweetened up and baked for shortcakes. For a flakier biscuit, I prefer to use cold, solid fat in this recipe but to be honest, liquid fat works perfectly well and is easier to add to the flour mixture. The quicker you make these and the less you work the dough, the lighter the biscuits will be.

2 cups Basic Pancake and Biscuit
Mix (page 18)
4 tablespoons (½ stick) cold,
unsalted butter or another fat

1 cup liquid (milk, dairy-free milk,
etc.)

Preheat the oven to 400 degrees. Line a baking sheet with parchment paper or a silicone baking mat.

Put the Basic Pancake and Muffin Mix in a large mixing bowl. Add the butter or other fat and cut the fat into the mix with a pastry cutter, two knives, or even your hands until the mixture resembles a coarse meal with some larger pieces of butter or fat. Add the liquid and stir with a fork just until combined.

For rolled biscuits, dust a work surface with some more of the baking mix, dump the dough on top, and knead 4 or 5 times. Flatten the dough with your hands into a disk about ¾ inch thick. Cut into circles with a 2-inch cookie cutter. Gather the dough scraps up, working the dough as little as possible, reshape into a disk, and cut the remaining dough. Place the biscuits on the prepared baking sheet and bake for 13 to 17 minutes, or until browned, firm to the touch, and a toothpick inserted in the center comes out clean.

For drop biscuits, simply spoon equal mounds of the dough (a little larger than a golf ball) onto the prepared baking sheet and bake 13 to 17 minutes, or

until browned, firm to the touch, and a toothpick inserted in the center comes out clean. The time will depend on the size of the biscuits.

VARIATIONS

Buttermilk Biscuits: Add 1 teaspoon of baking soda to the Basic Pancake and Biscuit Mix and mix well. Proceed as above using 1 cup buttermilk as the liquid. For dairy-free buttermilk, add 1 tablespoon fresh lemon juice or white vinegar to a cup of dairy-free milk, stir, and let sit for 5 minutes. Do not be alarmed if it looks a little curdled.

Dumplings: Prepare as for biscuits, drop spoonfuls of the batter on top of simmering stew or soup, cover the pan, and simmer for 10 to 15 minutes.

Shortcakes: Add ¼ cup sugar to the dough, prepare as for drop biscuits but make them larger (about 1½ times the size of biscuits, making 6 shortcakes), and sprinkle a little more sugar on top of each shortcake. Bake as for biscuits. When done, cut in half and top with fruit and whipped cream, if desired.

Whole Grain Pancake and Biscuit Mix

• Dairy-Free

Makes 8 cups mix

Just like the Basic Pancake and Biscuit Mix, this is a great basic mix to have on hand. The main difference is this mix is made with brown rice flour, which is a whole grain gluten-free flour. Pancakes and baked goods made with this mix will have a heartier taste and are healthier and more wholesome. Baked goods will not get quite as brown as those made with the Basic Mix, but they are still lovely and, of course, delicious.

As I stated in the recipe for Sweet Rice Flour Blend, not all flours are created equal. For the very best results use only superfine brown rice flour. My favorite brand is Authentic Foods, which is available in health food stores and on the Internet.

There is no xanthan or guar gum in this recipe as I find it unnecessary in this mix. You can vary the type of starch you add depending on other food sensitivities and personal taste preferences.

As with the Basic Pancake and Biscuit Mix, you have a wide variety of options regarding what type fat, sweetener, and liquid you use.

Make up a batch of this whole grain mix, store it in an airtight container in the pantry or in a plastic storage bag in the freezer, and you can get healthy pancakes or muffins on the table in no time with very little effort and lots of options.

6 cups superfine brown rice flour	8 teaspoons baking powder
2 cups tapioca starch (or potato or cornstarch)	4 teaspoons kosher or fine sea salt

In a large mixing bowl, slowly whisk all the ingredients together very well, making sure they are evenly distributed.

This recipe can easily be halved, doubled, or tripled.

Whole Grain Pancakes

A quick, healthy breakfast is easily prepared using Whole Grain Pancake and Biscuit Mix as a base. See Basic Pancakes (page 19) for ideas on how to customize this recipe to suit your own personal tastes. For fruit pancakes such as blueberry, stir in a cup of fruit after the batter has been whisked together.

• Dairy-Free Adaptable

Makes 12 pancakes

2 cups Whole Grain Pancake and Biscuit Mix (page 24)

2 large eggs

1 cup liquid (milk, dairy-free milk, etc.)

2 tablespoons liquid fat (melted butter, bacon grease, grapeseed, or coconut oil, etc.)

2 tablespoons sugar (or equivalent amount of another sweetener)

1 teaspoon pure vanilla extract

Whisk all the ingredients together in a large mixing bowl until fully combined and smooth. If adding fruit or other flavor agents, add them now.

Heat a skillet or griddle over medium heat until a drop of water sizzles immediately when splashed on the hot pan. Lightly grease the skillet with gluten-free, nonstick cooking spray, melted butter, or oil. Ladle ¼ cup of batter onto the pan for each pancake. Cook until the top of each pancake is bubbly, the edges appear dry, and the bottom is lightly browned, about 2 minutes. Flip and cook until the opposite side is browned, 1 to 2 minutes. Repeat with the remaining batter. The pancakes can be kept warm in a low (200-degree) oven until serving.

Whole Grain Muffins and Quick Breads

೧೧೧೧೧೧೧೧೧೧೧೧೧೧೧೧೧೧೧೧೧೧೧೧೧೧೧

• Dairy-Free
Adaptable

Healthy, whole grain, gluten-free muffins can be ready to eat in about 35 minutes, and make for a great start to any day. Muffins and quick breads also freeze well; just wrap them tightly in plastic wrap and warm up briefly before serving. Quick breads take longer to bake, but there is no effort required other than a little whisking and popping them in the oven.

2 cups Whole Grain Pancake and Biscuit Mix (page 24)	4 tablespoons ($\frac{1}{2}$ stick) unsalted butter, melted, or another fat
2 large eggs	$\frac{1}{4}$ cup sugar
1 cup liquid (milk, dairy-free milk, etc.)	1 teaspoon pure vanilla extract

Preheat the oven to 350 degrees. Line a 12-cup standard muffin pan with paper baking liners. For quick breads, spray a 9×5-inch loaf pan with gluten-free, nonstick cooking spray and line with a piece of parchment paper that hangs over the long sides of the pan. Spray the parchment paper lightly with cooking spray.

Put the Whole Grain Pancake and Biscuit Mix in a large mixing bowl. Break the eggs into another mixing bowl and whisk lightly. Add the remaining ingredients to the eggs and whisk to combine. Add the wet ingredients to the Whole Grain Pancake and Biscuit Mix and stir to combine. If you want to add fruit or other flavorings, do so after the batter has been whisked together. Divide the batter among the prepared muffin cups and bake for 25 to 30 minutes, or until a toothpick inserted into the center of a muffin comes out clean and the muffins are lightly browned. Muffins made with this mixture may not get as brown as those made with the Basic Pancake and Biscuit Mix. Let cool in the pan for 5 minutes then transfer to a wire rack to finish cooling.

For a quick bread, pour the batter into the prepared pan and bake for 50 to 60 minutes, or until a toothpick inserted into the center comes out clean and the top is lightly browned. Run a knife around the edges when it comes out of the oven. Let cool in the pan for 5 minutes, then transfer to a wire rack to finish cooling.

Makes 12 muffins or one 9 × 5-inch loaf

Note: For ideas of variations, see Basic Muffins and Quick Breads recipe (page 20).

Whole Grain Biscuits

- Dairy-Free Adaptable

- Vegetarian/ Vegan Adaptable

Healthy biscuits, dumplings, and shortcakes take just a few moments to prepare and have a wonderful, hearty flavor when prepared with the Whole Grain Pancake and Biscuit Mix. As with the Basic Biscuit dough, you want to work it as little as possible, and cold, solid fat is preferred to liquid (such as oil), but oil or other liquid fat will work in a pinch.

1½ cups Whole Grain Pancake and Biscuit Mix (page 24)
4 tablespoons (½ stick) cold, unsalted butter or another fat

½ cup liquid (milk, dairy-free milk, etc.)

Preheat the oven to 400 degrees. Line a baking sheet with parchment paper or a silicone baking mat.

Put the Whole Grain Pancake and Biscuit Mix in a large mixing bowl. Add the butter or other fat and cut the fat into the mix with a pastry cutter, two knives, or even your hands until the mixture resembles a coarse meal with some larger pieces of butter or fat. Add the liquid and stir with a fork just until combined.

For rolled biscuits, dust a work surface with some more baking mix, dump the dough on top, and knead 4 or 5 times. Flatten the dough with your hands into a disk about ¾ inch thick. Cut into circles with a 2-inch cookie cutter. Gather the dough scraps up, working the dough as little as possible, reshape into a disk, and cut the remaining dough. Place the biscuits on the prepared baking sheet and bake for 15 to 20 minutes, or until browned, firm to the touch, and a toothpick inserted in the center comes out clean.

For drop biscuits, simply spoon equal mounds of the dough onto the prepared baking sheet and bake 15 to 20 minutes, or until browned, firm to the touch,

and a toothpick inserted in the center comes out clean. Time will depend on the size of the biscuits.

VARIATIONS

Dumplings: Prepare as for biscuits, drop spoonfuls of the batter on top of simmering stew or soup, cover the pan, and simmer for 15 to 20 minutes.

Shortcakes: Add ¼ cup sugar to the dough, prepare as for drop biscuits, and sprinkle a little more sugar on top of each shortcake. Bake as for biscuits. When done, cut in half, top with fruit and whipped cream, if desired.

Simple Suppers

ONE OF THE BIGGEST challenges we face in these busy times is getting food on the table fast that is both tasty and nutritious.

When my boys were growing up, I worked full-time. They had school and activities, and we would often arrive home at 6:00 p.m. The children were hungry and cranky, needed to be fed, get their homework done, bathe, and get to bed. I didn't have the luxury of taking hours to prepare dinner.

Yet as hectic as life was, we always sat down for dinner at the table and ate together as a family. It was often the only time we had to connect during the day. The best way I can think to get everyone to the table is to offer a variety of delicious food.

These simple suppers are simple in the sense that they are easy and quick to prepare, most using readily available ingredients, but they certainly are not simple in flavor. We can circle the globe with these weekday meals.

These are full dinners that are designed to be ready in about half an hour. I say "about half an hour" because everyone has different skill levels, uses different kitchen equipment, and works at different speeds. And, of course, necessity plays a role; I know I work a whole lot faster when I have crabby kids screaming for dinner than when I am all alone on a Sunday afternoon preparing a meal.

In this chapter, I give you weekday dinners with quick-cooking strategies to get the whole meal on the table at the same time. You can apply many of these same principles to other menus. As with all my menus and recipes, my hope is to not just give you a set menu that must be followed to the letter but also one that you can use as a springboard. By adapting the menus to include your own personal favorites, you add your own creativity and flair, making these recipes your own.

All-American Meat Loaf Dinner

• Dairy-Free

MENU

Mini Meat Loaves

Dairy-Free, Ranch-Style Smashed Potatoes

Broccoli with Garlic Chips

Dairy-Free Chocolate Ganache with Fruit

Meat loaf just cries out "home-cooked comfort" to me. By baking the meat loaves in muffin pans, the baking time decreases from 1 hour to about 20 minutes. And what goes better with meat loaf than mashed potatoes and broccoli? The potato recipe has the flavor of buttermilk ranch dressing without the dairy. The dairy-free dressing adds a little zing to plain old mashed potatoes and is great as a salad dressing all on its own. The broccoli is ready in just a few minutes and the garlic slivers give it a little panache.

To my mind, there is not much in this world better than chocolate—except maybe something dipped in chocolate. This quick, dairy-free chocolate ganache makes a fun dessert. Serve it in individual bowls with whatever fruit you have on hand for dipping: strawberries, apples, bananas, and even orange segments make great dippers.

Quick-Cook Strategy

- Preheat the oven to 450 degrees and start the potatoes boiling in a large pot of water on the stovetop.
- Grating the onion and carrot on a box grater for the meat loaves is faster than chopping them and has the added benefit of making the meat loaves moister. If you have a microplane grater, grate the garlic for the meat loaves on that instead of mincing. Grate the garlic for the potatoes at the same time.
- Use Yukon Gold potatoes. They have thin skins, so you can skip peeling them, which not only makes the meal come together faster, it also makes it more nutritious as many nutrients are contained in the skins. And remember, a covered pot will boil faster.
- While the meat loaves are in the oven and the potatoes are boiling, you will have a little pocket of time to prepare the sauce for the potatoes and make the ganache.
- The ganache will thicken as it cools. To speed this process up, just pop it into the freezer for about 10 minutes.
- The Broccoli with Garlic Chips only takes a few minutes so make that last.
- Using bags of broccoli florets saves tons of time.

Mini Meat Loaves

1½ pounds lean ground sirloin

1 small or ½ large white onion

1 carrot

2 garlic cloves

1 teaspoon kosher or fine sea salt

½ teaspoon freshly ground black
   pepper

1 tablespoon Worcestershire
   sauce, plus a couple of dashes
   for the glaze

1 cup gluten-free bread
   crumbs

1 large egg

⅓ cup ketchup

Dash of hot sauce

2 teaspoons honey

Preheat the oven to 450 degrees. Spray a standard muffin pan with gluten-free, nonstick cooking spray.

Put the ground sirloin in a large mixing bowl. Grate in the onion, carrot, and garlic. Add the salt, pepper, Worcestershire sauce, bread crumbs, and egg. Mix with your hands to combine. Do not overmix the ingredients. Portion the mixture into the prepared muffin pan; an ice cream scoop works well for this, or just lightly roll the meat mixture into balls with your hands.

In a small bowl, combine the ketchup with a couple dashes of Worcestershire sauce, the hot sauce, and the honey. Spoon some on top of each mini meat loaf. Bake for 18 to 20 minutes. To make sure they are cooked through, cut into one mini loaf; the meat should no longer be pink.

Dairy-Free, Ranch-Style Smashed Potatoes

2 pounds Yukon Gold potatoes

½ cup coconut milk (or dairy-free milk of your choice)

Juice of 1 lemon

1 small garlic clove, minced or grated

1 teaspoon finely chopped flat-leaf parsley

1 teaspoon finely chopped chives or scallion

½ teaspoon freshly ground black pepper

2 tablespoons good-quality, dairy-free butter substitute (such as Earth Balance)

Kosher or fine sea salt

Scrub the potatoes and cut them roughly into 1-inch pieces. Add to a large pot of salted water, cover, and bring to a boil. Cook until tender, about 15 minutes.

While the potatoes are boiling, make the ranch dressing. In a small bowl or measuring cup, combine the coconut milk and lemon juice. Let sit for 5 minutes; if it becomes a little curdled, that is fine. Add the garlic, parsley, chives, and black pepper and stir to combine.

When the potatoes are tender, drain and return them to the hot pot. Smash with a potato masher or handheld mixer. Add the dairy-free butter and stir to melt and combine. Mix in the dressing. Taste and add more salt, if needed.

Broccoli with Garlic Chips

1 pound broccoli florets	½ teaspoon kosher or fine sea
2 tablespoons olive oil	salt
2 garlic cloves, peeled and thinly	½ teaspoon freshly ground black
sliced	pepper

Bring a large pot of salted water to a boil over high heat. When the water boils, add the broccoli and cook until almost tender, but still crisp, 2 to 3 minutes. Drain and set aside.

Heat the olive oil in the same pot over medium heat. Add the sliced garlic and cook, stirring, until the garlic starts to soften and brown lightly, about 2 minutes. Return the broccoli to the pot, season with salt and pepper, and toss gently to combine.

Dairy-Free Chocolate Ganache with Fruit

1 cup dairy-free chocolate chips

½ cup coconut milk (or dairy-free milk of your choice)

1 tablespoon pure vanilla extract

1 tablespoon good-quality, dairy-free butter substitute (such as Earth Balance)

Whole berries, sliced apples, banana chunks, orange segments, or whatever fruit you prefer; plan on about 1 piece of whole fruit or a large handful of berries per person

Place the chocolate chips, coconut milk, and vanilla in a microwave-safe bowl. Microwave on high power for 2 minutes, or until most of the chocolate is melted. Stir the mixture until all the chocolate is melted and the mixture is smooth and glossy. Add the dairy-free butter substitute and stir to combine. Set aside until ready to serve. The mixture will thicken as it sits. To speed up this process, put the ganache in the freezer for 10 minutes, then give it a good stir before serving with the fruit.

Rustic Elegance

∽∽∽∽∽∽∽∽

MENU

Ricotta and Tomato Pasta

Rustic Salad

Blitzed Brownies

∽∽∽∽∽∽∽∽

This pasta dish is a lighter, more elegant, deconstructed version of lasagna; all the flavors with a fraction of the time and effort. Serve the pasta in individual bowls with a dollop of the ricotta mixture. It is a pretty, rustic presentation and allows the diner to mix in a bit of the ricotta with each bite.

The flourless brownies are ready in less than half an hour, and have endless possibilities. Change the nuts and dried fruit to suit your own taste.

Quick-Cook Strategy

- Start the water boiling for the pasta in a large pan with a lid. Preheat the oven.
- Prepare the brownies and get them in the oven. If you have not taken the butter out of the refrigerator ahead of time, you can soften it in the microwave on 30 percent power for about 30 seconds, but watch carefully, microwaves cook from the inside out and the center can liquefy.

Serves 4 (with plenty of leftover brownies for later)

- The recipe makes plenty of brownies, so you will have dessert or treats for another day. They are good warm from the oven or cold; a scoop of ice cream is a nice addition.
- Once the brownies are in the oven, slice up the bacon and get it frying, cut up the bread and lettuce for the salad, halve the tomatoes for the pasta, and make the salad dressing. Then get on to the rest of the pasta recipe.

Ricotta and Tomato Pasta

14 ounces gluten-free, fettuccine-style rice pasta

¾ cup ricotta cheese (preferably fresh)

¼ cup finely grated Parmesan cheese, plus more for garnish

½ teaspoon dried oregano

Kosher or fine sea salt

Freshly ground black pepper

2 tablespoons olive oil, plus extra for drizzling

2 garlic cloves, minced

2 pints grape or cherry tomatoes, halved

Pinch of crushed red pepper flakes

2 cups baby spinach leaves

Bring a large pot of salted water to a boil and cook the pasta until al dente. Reserve ½ cup of the pasta cooking water and drain the pasta. Return the drained pasta to the hot pot.

While the pasta is cooking, prepare the cheese mixture and the sauce. In a small mixing bowl, combine the ricotta cheese with the ¼ cup grated Parmesan cheese, the dried oregano, and a large pinch of salt and pepper. Set aside.

Heat the 2 tablespoons of olive oil in a large skillet over medium-high heat until hot. Add the garlic and cook, stirring, for 30 seconds. Do not let the garlic brown. Add the tomatoes, red pepper flakes, 1 teaspoon salt, and ½ teaspoon black pepper. Cook for 4 minutes, then add the reserved pasta water and spinach. Cook for another minute or two, or until the spinach has wilted.

Add the tomato-spinach mixture to the pasta in the pot and toss to combine. Serve the pasta in large, shallow bowls with a dollop of the ricotta mixture in the center. Drizzle with a little olive oil and sprinkle with additional finely grated Parmesan cheese.

Rustic Salad

7 tablespoons olive oil

5 slices thick-cut bacon, sliced
crosswise into ½-inch pieces

4 slices gluten-free sandwich
bread, cut into ½-inch cubes

2 tablespoons red wine vinegar

1 tablespoon Dijon mustard

Kosher or fine sea salt

Freshly ground black pepper

2 hearts romaine lettuce,
coarsely chopped

Place a large skillet over medium-high heat and add 1 tablespoon of the olive oil. Once the oil is hot, add the sliced bacon. Cook, stirring occasionally, until the slices start to brown and have rendered out some fat, about 3 minutes. Reduce the heat to medium and add the bread cubes, tossing to coat them in the bacon fat. Spread the bread cubes out in the pan so they brown evenly, and cook, stirring occasionally, until browned and crispy, about 4 minutes. Set aside in the pan until ready to toss with the lettuce.

Combine the remaining 6 tablespoons of olive oil with the vinegar, Dijon mustard, and a good pinch of salt and pepper in a small jar and shake well. Just before serving, put the lettuce in a salad bowl, toss with the dressing, add the reserved bacon and bread cubes, and give it another gentle toss.

Blitzed Brownies

1¼ cups good-quality bittersweet chocolate chips
1 cup (2 sticks) unsalted butter,
  softened
4 large eggs
1 cup sugar
6 tablespoons unsweetened
  cocoa powder
2 tablespoons cornstarch
½ teaspoon kosher or fine sea salt

1 tablespoon instant espresso
  powder (optional)
2 teaspoons pure vanilla extract
¼ cup coarsely chopped dried
  apricots
¼ cup coarsely chopped dried
  cherries
¼ cup coarsely chopped roasted
  pistachios

Preheat the oven to 375 degrees. Line a 12×9-inch baking dish with parchment paper.

Put the chocolate chips and butter in the bowl of a food processor fitted with the steel blade. Pulse a few times to roughly combine. Add the eggs, sugar, cocoa powder, cornstarch, salt, espresso powder, and vanilla and process until combined. There will be small bits of chocolate in the mix; that's fine. Spread the mixture into the prepared baking dish and smooth out the top. Sprinkle the chopped fruit and nuts over the top and gently press into the batter. Bake the brownies for 20 minutes, or until the batter looks completely set and feels slightly firm to the touch. The outer edges will be a little drier than the inside.

For a rustic presentation, remove the parchment paper from the baking dish, along with the brownies, and set it on a cutting board. Cut into squares and serve. Leftover brownies can be wrapped in plastic wrap and stored in the refrigerator for several days.

• Dairy-Free

Asian-Inspired Salmon and Rice

◈◈◈◈◈◈◈◈◈

MENU

Glazed Salmon

Brown Rice with Edamame

Spicy Quick Pickles

◈◈◈◈◈◈◈◈◈

This salmon recipe will give you an instant reputation as a gourmet chef and yet nothing could be simpler. Serve the salmon on top of Brown Rice with Edamame to soak up the luscious sauce.

Versions of quick pickles showed up on my dinner table often when I was a child. Usually they were as simple as cucumber, salt, pepper, vinegar, and a touch of sugar. Here I have added a bit of Asian flare as well as some heat.

This is a light, quick meal that is as good for you as it is good. If you need some dessert, store-bought sherbet or some chilled, canned lychee nuts would be perfect.

In the event of leftovers, you can flake the salmon and toss it along with everything else and refrigerate; it makes a delicious salad for the next day's lunch.

Quick-Cook Strategy

- Make the quick pickles first as they can stand for as little as 10 minutes or up to an hour. If you prepare the pickles in a container with a secure lid, you can just shake the mixture a few times, saving you from having to stir them.
- Start the rice next as it takes the longest. I don't even start the salmon until the rice has been cooked and set aside. That way, I can get everything on the table, stress-free.

Glazed Salmon

¼ cup mirin (Japanese sweet rice wine)	Four 4-ounce salmon fillets, skin removed
¼ cup gluten-free soy sauce	1 tablespoon rice wine vinegar
¼ cup firmly packed brown sugar	2 scallions, finely sliced on the diagonal
1 teaspoon sesame oil	

In a shallow baking dish, combine the mirin, soy sauce, brown sugar, and sesame oil. Add the salmon fillets and let marinate for 3 minutes. Flip and let marinate on the other side.

Heat a large skillet over medium-high heat. Add the salmon fillets and cook for 2 minutes. Turn the fillets over and cook for another 2 minutes. Transfer to a serving dish. Add the marinade to the hot skillet. Add the rice wine vinegar and cook, stirring, until it reduces slightly, about 2 minutes. Pour the sauce over the salmon, garnish with the sliced scallions, and serve immediately.

Brown Rice with Edamame

1³/₄ cups water	2 teaspoons sesame oil
¹/₂ teaspoon kosher or fine sea salt	¹/₂ teaspoon sugar
2 teaspoons gluten-free soy sauce	1 cup instant brown rice
2 tablespoons rice wine vinegar	1 cup frozen shelled edamame, thawed
	1 tablespoon sesame seeds

Combine the water, salt, soy sauce, rice wine vinegar, sesame oil, sugar, and rice in a medium saucepan and bring to a boil. Cover the pan, reduce the heat to medium-low, and simmer, covered, for 10 to 12 minutes, or until all the liquid has been absorbed. Fluff the rice with a fork and add the thawed edamame. Replace the cover and let sit in the pan for 5 minutes. Add the sesame seeds and give the rice a final fluff with a fork. Serve immediately.

Spicy Quick Pickles

¼ cup rice vinegar

2 teaspoons gluten-free soy
   sauce

1 tablespoon sugar

½ teaspoon freshly ground black
   pepper

½ teaspoon crushed red pepper
   flakes

2 small cucumbers, peeled and
   thinly sliced

In a medium mixing bowl, stir together the vinegar, soy sauce, sugar, black pepper, and red pepper flakes until the sugar has dissolved. Add the cucumber slices and toss to coat. Cover and let refrigerate for 10 minutes or up to an hour, stirring occasionally.

Weeknight Mexican Fiesta

• Dairy-Free
Adaptable

MENU

Enchilada Lasagna

Orange and Red Onion Salad

South-of-the-Border Sundaes

The Enchilada Lasagna has all the flavor of enchiladas without all the rolling and fuss. Many canned enchilada sauces contain gluten, but not to worry, this is a quick, homemade version you can make almost as fast as you can open a can.

Quick-Cook Strategy

- Buying low-fat ground turkey saves not only calories but also time; the less fat the faster it browns.
- While the turkey is browning, whip up the sauce in the blender.
- Preshredded cheese will make this meal come together faster.
- Pop the coconut flakes into the oven at the same time as the Enchilada Lasagna but watch them, they go from a lovely toasted brown to burnt in the blink of an eye. If you want, make a little extra toasted coconut and sprinkle in the salad.

Serves 6

- Make the pineapple topping for the sundaes while the Enchilada Lasagna is baking.
- You can prepare the salad up to the point of adding the lettuce and set it aside. Toss in the lettuce just before serving.

Enchilada Lasagna

2 tablespoons olive oil

1 large onion, chopped

2 pounds ground turkey

One 14.5-ounce can fire-roasted
   tomatoes

One 4.5-ounce can chopped mild
   green chilies

1½ teaspoons ground cumin

1 teaspoon kosher or fine sea salt

½ teaspoon freshly ground black
   pepper

1 tablespoon red chili powder

One 15-ounce can black beans,
   rinsed and drained

8 corn tortillas

4 cups shredded sharp cheddar
   cheese or Mexican cheese
   blend (or dairy-free cheese)

One 4-ounce can sliced black
   olives, drained

2 scallions, sliced diagonally

¼ cup fresh cilantro leaves

½ cup sour cream (or dairy-free
   sour cream) for serving

½ cup prepared chunky salsa for
   serving

Preheat the oven to 425 degrees. Spray a shallow, 9×9-inch baking dish with gluten-free, nonstick cooking spray.

Heat the olive oil in a large skillet over medium-high heat. Add the onion and cook until it starts to soften, about 5 minutes. Remove half of the onion and place in the jar of a blender. Add the turkey to the remaining onion, breaking it up as you brown it, about 5 minutes. While the meat is browning, make the sauce.

Add the canned tomatoes, including the juice, along with the chilies, cumin, salt, pepper, and chili powder to the onion in the blender. Process until pureed. If the sauce is too thick, add some water, a tablespoon at a time; it should be thick. Drain any excess fat from the browned turkey, and add the sauce to the pan. Add the black beans and cook for 2 to 3 minutes, or until everything is heated through.

Cut the tortillas into quarters. Add half the turkey mixture to the prepared dish. Top with half the tortilla quarters and then half the cheese. Repeat the layering, and top with the sliced black olives. Bake for 12 to 15 minutes, or until the cheese is browned and bubbly. Top with the scallions and cilantro leaves. Serve with sour cream and salsa on the side.

Orange and Red Onion Salad

1 tablespoon orange marmalade	½ small red onion, thinly sliced
2 tablespoons red wine vinegar	2 hearts romaine lettuce,
⅓ cup olive oil	chopped
One 11-ounce can mandarin	Kosher or fine sea salt
orange segments, drained	Freshly ground black pepper

In a salad bowl, combine the orange marmalade with the red wine vinegar. Whisk in the olive oil. Add the drained orange segments and sliced red onion. Just before serving, add the chopped romaine and toss to coat. Season to taste with salt and pepper. Serve immediately.

South-of-the-Border Sundaes

½ cup sweetened coconut flakes

2 tablespoons unsalted butter or dairy-free butter substitute

½ cup firmly packed brown sugar

¼ teaspoon kosher or fine sea salt

One 20-ounce can pineapple tidbits in juice

1 tablespoon dark rum (or 1 teaspoon pure vanilla extract)

Vanilla or coconut store-bought ice cream or dairy-free ice cream

Preheat the oven to 425 degrees.

Place the coconut in a layer in a pie pan or on a baking sheet. Toast in the oven until lightly browned and fragrant, about 5 minutes. Remove from the oven and let cool.

Melt the butter in a large skillet over medium-high heat. Add the brown sugar and salt and cook until the sugar has dissolved. Add the pineapple pieces along with their juice and the rum (or vanilla) and cook until the liquid has reduced by half, 5 to 6 minutes. Let cool slightly. If making the sauce ahead, re-warm slightly before serving.

Scoop the ice cream into individual bowls and top with pineapple sauce and toasted coconut. Serve immediately.

Greek Burgers and Fries

MENU

Greek Burgers

Quick Tzatziki Sauce

Lemon-Roasted Fingerling Potatoes

Greek Salad

Cheater's Rice Pudding

This is a Greek version of the all-American dinner—burgers and fries. Lamb and Greek potatoes show up on the menu in simplified recipes and there is even a quick recipe for rice pudding, which uses a cheat of instant rice, but leftover cooked rice would work also. Instead of gluten-free buns, the burgers are placed on portobello mushroom caps that are not only naturally gluten-free but also so much more flavorful. Use some of the tzatziki sauce to top the burgers and serve the rest for dipping the potatoes.

Serves 4

Quick-Cook Strategy

- Preheat the oven for the potatoes and get the rice pudding started first thing. The rice pudding doesn't require much attention other than an occasional stir.
- As soon as the pudding is cooking, slice the potatoes and get them in the oven. Next make the tzatziki sauce so it has time to sit, allowing the flavors to meld.
- The repeated use of ingredients like feta cheese and cucumbers makes it easier to shop for the meal.
- Using Greek-style yogurt is essential to making the tzatziki sauce quickly. Traditional yogurt needs to be strained for hours or it will make the sauce watery.
- Hothouse cucumbers have fewer seeds than the typical garden cucumbers so try to get those, if you can, to avoid having to remove the seeds for the tzatziki sauce. If you can't get hothouse cucumbers, then cut the cucumber in half and scrape out the seeds with a spoon; the seeds will also make the sauce watery.

Greek Burgers

1½ pounds ground lamb

4 ounces feta cheese, crumbled

1 teaspoon dried oregano

½ teaspoon kosher or fine
    sea salt, plus more for
    seasoning

¼ teaspoon freshly ground
    black pepper, plus more for
    seasoning

Olive oil

4 large portobello mushroom
    caps

Combine the ground lamb, feta cheese, oregano, ½ teaspoon salt, and ¼ teaspoon pepper in a mixing bowl and mix well. Divide the mixture into 4 equal portions and shape into patties about ¾ inch thick. With your thumb, make a shallow indentation in the center of each burger; this will ensure even cooking and keep the burger flat. Brush both sides of the patties with a little olive oil and sprinkle with a bit of salt and pepper.

If there is still a woody part of the stem left in the mushroom caps, cut that out with a paring knife. Brush both sides of the mushroom caps with some olive oil and season with a little salt and pepper.

Heat a large skillet with a lid over high heat. Place the mushroom caps into the skillet, gill-side up. Grill for 1½ to 2 minutes, flip over and grill the opposite side for another 1½ to 2 minutes. Transfer the mushroom caps to a serving platter or four individual plates.

Reduce the heat to medium, place the patties in the skillet, cover, and cook for 3 to 4 minutes on each side, or until firm to the touch. Place the cooked patties on top of the mushroom caps and top with a dollop of tzatziki sauce.

Quick Tzatziki Sauce

½ hothouse cucumber, peeled and grated using the large holes on a box grater

2 garlic cloves, minced or grated on a microplane grater

¾ cup plain Greek yogurt

¼ cup sour cream

½ teaspoon kosher or fine sea salt

½ teaspoon freshly ground black pepper

2 tablespoons minced fresh dill

Mix all the ingredients together in a mixing bowl, cover with plastic wrap, and refrigerate until ready to serve.

Lemon-Roasted Fingerling Potatoes

1½ pounds fingerling potatoes, sliced in half lengthwise

Juice of 1 lemon

2 tablespoons olive oil

1 teaspoon kosher or fine sea salt

½ teaspoon freshly ground black pepper

½ teaspoon garlic powder

Preheat the oven to 450 degrees.

Place the potatoes on a rimmed baking sheet, top with the remaining ingredients, and toss to coat. Spread the potatoes out in a single layer and roast for 15 to 20 minutes, or until the potatoes are crispy, turning the potatoes once halfway through the cooking time.

Greek Salad

2 tablespoons red wine vinegar

1/2 teaspoon kosher or fine sea salt

1/4 teaspoon freshly ground black pepper

1 teaspoon dried oregano

6 tablespoons good extra-virgin olive oil

2 large tomatoes

1 1/2 hothouse cucumbers, peeled and cut into 1-inch chunks

1/2 small red onion, halved and thinly sliced

4 ounces feta cheese, diced into 1/2-inch pieces

1/2 cup pitted black kalamata olives

In the bottom of a salad bowl, whisk together the vinegar, salt, pepper, and oregano. Slowly whisk in the olive oil.

Cut the tomatoes in half crosswise and gently squeeze out the seeds. Cut into 1/2-inch pieces. Add to the dressing along with the remaining salad ingredients and gently toss to coat everything with the dressing. Taste and add additional salt and pepper, if needed. Serve immediately.

Cheater's Rice Pudding

2½ cups whole milk

2 cups instant white rice

½ teaspoon kosher or fine sea
   salt

¼ cup honey

1 teaspoon pure vanilla extract

½ cup heavy whipping cream
   (optional)

Ground cinnamon for garnish

Combine the milk, rice, salt, honey, and vanilla in a medium saucepan with a lid. Bring to a boil, cover, and reduce the heat to low. Cook, stirring occasionally, for 20 minutes, or until the milk has been completely absorbed and the rice is tender. For a creamier pudding, stir in the heavy cream as soon as the pudding is done. Serve warm topped with a dusting of ground cinnamon.

Quick Comfort

∽∽∽∽∽∽∽∽∽

MENU

Quick Mac and Cheese

Baked Tomatoes

Instant Berry Frozen Yogurt

∽∽∽∽∽∽∽∽∽

Some days just cry out for comfort food, something that nourishes the soul as well as feeds the body. To my way of thinking, there is nothing more comforting than macaroni and cheese. The beauty of gluten-free macaroni and cheese is that it is actually easier to prepare than the traditional; no making a roux by cooking flour and butter together. The world seems to be equally split when it comes to a preference of creamy mac and cheese versus baked. This recipe offers an optional step of adding a crunchy topping for those that prefer more of a baked variety.

As a child I smothered my mac and cheese with ketchup. These days I prefer to eat it alongside Baked Tomatoes for that tomato tang. If your idea of comfort includes salad, feel free to add a simple tossed green salad.

Ice cream is another favorite comfort food but in concession to all the cheese in this meal I offer you a quick, low-calorie berry frozen yogurt that is just as tasty as any ice cream. The method of preparing the frozen yogurt in this recipe works just as well with other frozen fruits.

Quick-Cook Strategy

Serves 6

- Start the water boiling for the pasta in a large pan with a lid. Preheat the oven.
- While the pasta is cooking, you have a stretch of time where you can whip up the sauce, prepare the tomatoes, and get the cheese sauce done.
- I timed myself to see how long it took me to shred the cheese by hand using a box grater. It took exactly 90 seconds. If you haven't got an extra 90 seconds then by all means feel free to use preshredded cheese.
- If I am making the crunchy-topped version of the mac and cheese with the Baked Tomatoes, I prepare the topping for both at the same time: mix the cheese, bread crumbs, and olive oil together; take out half the mixture for the mac and cheese; then add the seasoning for the tomatoes. This saves time and another bowl to clean.
- The Instant Berry Frozen Yogurt is ready in a minute, so make this while someone else is clearing the dinner dishes away.

Quick Mac and Cheese

12 ounces gluten-free macaroni

3 cups low-fat (2 percent) milk

2 tablespoons cornstarch

½ teaspoon kosher or sea salt

½ teaspoon freshly ground black
pepper

3 dashes hot sauce

2 cups sharp cheddar cheese,
grated on the large holes of a
box grater

½ cup Gruyère cheese, grated
on the large holes of a box
grater

OPTIONAL CRUNCHY TOPPING

¼ cup grated Parmesan cheese

¼ cup gluten-free, panko-style
bread crumbs

2 tablespoons olive oil

If making the crunchy-topped version, preheat the oven to 500 degrees.

Cook the macaroni according to the package directions. When the pasta is done, drain it well and return it to the hot pot.

While the pasta is cooking, prepare the sauce. Mix ¼ cup of the milk with the cornstarch and stir well to combine. Heat the remaining milk with the salt, pepper, and hot sauce in a large, deep saucepan just until it comes to a boil. Whisk in the cornstarch mixture and cook for about 1 minute, stirring constantly, until the mixture has thickened. Remove from the heat, add the cheeses, and stir until melted. Add the cheese sauce to the cooked pasta and mix well.

If you are including the crunchy topping, pour the mixture into a shallow baking dish. Combine the topping ingredients and spread over the top of the mac and cheese. Bake in the oven for 6 to 7 minutes or until the topping is golden brown.

Baked Tomatoes

6 large beefsteak tomatoes

Dijon mustard

¼ cup gluten-free, panko-style
    bread crumbs (or just toast a
    slice of gluten-free bread and
    give it a whiz in the blender to
    make your own)

2 tablespoons olive oil

¼ cup grated Parmesan cheese

½ teaspoon kosher or fine sea
    salt

½ teaspoon freshly ground black
    pepper

1 teaspoon dried oregano

½ teaspoon garlic powder

Preheat the oven to 500 degrees.

Cut the tomatoes in half crosswise. Spread the cut side of each half with a thin layer of Dijon mustard. In a small mixing bowl, combine the remaining ingredients. Press mixture onto the tomatoes and bake for 6 to 7 minutes, or until the tops are browned and the tomatoes are starting to soften.

Instant Berry Frozen Yogurt

Two 12-ounce bags frozen berries (blueberries, strawberries, raspberries, or mixed berries)
Juice of 1 large lemon

Two 17.6-ounce containers of Greek yogurt (full fat, nonfat, or fat free)
4 to 6 tablespoons honey

Place the frozen berries in the bowl of a food processor fitted with a steel blade and pulse several times to break up the berries. Add the lemon juice, yogurt, and 4 tablespoons of the honey. Process the mixture, scraping down the bowl 3 or 4 times, until smooth and completely combined. Taste and add more honey if desired. Serve immediately in glasses or dessert bowls.

Pie for Dinner

• Dairy-Free Adaptable

MENU

Polenta Potpies

Pear and Arugula Salad

Hot Cherry Sundaes

Even if we could find good gluten-free, frozen potpies, they would take just as long to bake as these homemade polenta potpies, and the polenta adds much more flavor than a regular crust topping. Using either leftover roasted chicken or a store-bought rotisserie chicken is the trick to making this dish in a flash. This is also a great way to use up leftover cooked vegetables; just toss them into the potpie as well.

When served over vanilla ice cream (or dairy-free ice cream), the hot cherry sauce is like a quick, nonalcoholic take on Cherries Jubilee. For a Black Forest version try it over chocolate ice cream instead.

Quick-Cook Strategy

- Using a large skillet or Dutch oven helps make the sauce for the polenta pies cook faster.
- If using cheese in the Polenta Potpies, preshredded will save time.

Serves 4

- Prepare the pecans, pears, and dressing for the salad while the sauce for the potpies is cooking. The pears can sit in the dressing until ready to toss with the arugula just before serving. Buying bagged, prewashed baby arugula saves time.
- You can also prepare the hot cherry sauce while the potpie sauce is cooking, and leave it in the pan until ready to serve dessert. If the sauce cools down too much, just reheat it gently for a minute or two.

Polenta Potpies

1 tablespoon cornstarch

3 cups gluten-free chicken stock

2 teaspoons olive oil

2 carrots, chopped

Kosher or fine sea salt

Freshly ground black pepper

1 cup cream or coconut milk

3 cups chopped cooked chicken

1 cup frozen baby onions

1 tablespoon minced fresh
   rosemary

1 cup frozen peas

³/₄ cup instant polenta

1 cup grated cheese (I prefer
   Gruyère) (optional if making
   dairy-free)

Mix the cornstarch with ¼ cup of the chicken stock and set aside.

In a large skillet or Dutch oven, warm the olive oil over medium-high heat and then add the chopped carrots. Season with salt and pepper and cook until the carrots just start to caramelize, about 5 minutes. Add 1 ¾ cups of the chicken stock, ½ cup of the cream or coconut milk, chopped chicken, frozen onions, and minced rosemary and bring to a simmer. (You can also add any leftover cooked veggies you may have on hand; butternut squash or potatoes are particularly good.) Let simmer about 15 minutes. The veggies should be tender and the chicken heated through. Add the frozen peas. Increase the heat, bring the mixture to a boil, and stir in the cornstarch mixture. Boil for 1 minute, then remove from the heat. Taste the mixture and adjust seasoning, if needed. Divide the mixture among four ovenproof bowls or ramekins and set them on a baking sheet.

Preheat the broiler and place the oven rack in the middle position.

In a saucepan over medium-high heat, bring the remaining 1 cup of chicken stock and the remaining ½ cup of cream or coconut milk to a boil. Gradually whisk in the polenta and cook until thick, about 3 minutes. Reduce the heat to low and stir in the cheese, if using, until melted.

Top the chicken mixture with the polenta and smooth it. Place in the broiler for 2 to 3 minutes, or until the tops are browned.

Pear and Arugula Salad

½ cup pecans

¼ cup olive oil

2 tablespoons freshly squeezed
   lemon juice

1 teaspoon honey

½ teaspoon kosher or fine sea salt

¼ teaspoon freshly ground black
   pepper

2 pears, peeled, cored, and thinly
   sliced

5 cups baby arugula

Place the pecans in a dry skillet and toast over medium-high heat until fragrant and lightly toasted, 4 to 5 minutes. Set aside to cool.

Whisk together the olive oil, lemon juice, honey, salt, and pepper in the bottom of a salad bowl. Add the pears and toss gently to combine.

Just before serving, add the arugula and toss to coat with the dressing. Taste and add additional salt and pepper, if needed. Top with the toasted pecans and serve.

Hot Cherry Sundaes

One 15-ounce can pitted dark
    sweet cherries in heavy syrup
1 tablespoon unsalted butter or
    good-quality, nondairy butter
    substitute (such as Earth
    Balance)
1 tablespoon cornstarch or
    arrowroot powder

Zest of 1 medium orange
1 tablespoon freshly squeezed
    orange juice
1 teaspoon pure vanilla extract
1½ pints store-bought ice cream
    or dairy-free ice cream

Drain the cherries and reserve the juice.

In a medium skillet over medium heat, melt the butter or butter substitute. Add the cornstarch or arrowroot powder and whisk until completely smooth. Add the reserved cherry juice and whisk constantly until the mixture has thickened, about 1 minute. Add the cherries, orange zest, orange juice, and vanilla. Reduce the heat to low and cook, stirring gently, until the cherries are heated through, 1 to 2 minutes. Serve over scoops of ice cream.

Curry in a Hurry

- Dairy-Free

- Vegetarian/ Vegan

MENU

Vegetable Curry

Spiced Basmati Rice with Cashews

Dairy-Free Mango Lassis

My mother grew up in India and made curry so hot and spicy that tears would roll down my face when I ate it, and my sinuses were cleared for weeks. This curry recipe is not as scorching hot, but if that's the way you like it, just add more curry paste. Conversely, if you like yours milder, add less. The basmati rice soaks up the curry sauce and, if desired, some jarred mango chutney served on the side will round out this vegetarian meal. If you believe no meal is complete without meat, chop or shred some cooked chicken or other meat and add to the curry.

A *lassi* is an Indian dessert drink similar to a milk shake typically made with mango, yogurt, ice, and milk. I make mine dairy-free and use frozen mango chunks that I don't even bother thawing. My husband, who is a dairy lover, prefers the dairy-free version to the original because the dairy masks the full flavor of the mango.

Quick-Cook Strategy

- There is no crime in buying precut squash and packaged cauliflower florets, it saves heaps of time. Get the veggies going for the curry and then start the rice.
- Toasting the rice not only adds flavor but also helps it cook faster. If you prefer plain rice, then you can make it in the microwave, increase the water to 3 cups, combine with the rice and salt in a covered, microwave-safe dish, and cook on high power for 5 minutes, then 50 percent power for 20 minutes. Let the rice stand for 5 minutes, then fluff with a fork.
- The *lassis* are so quick, you can whip them up in just seconds between clearing the table from dinner and serving dessert, or serve them with dinner, no one will mind!

Vegetable Curry

2 tablespoons olive oil

4 cups butternut squash, peeled, seeded, and cubed

1 large Idaho potato, peeled and cubed

1 medium yellow or white onion, thinly sliced

One 12-ounce bag cauliflower florets

2 to 4 tablespoons gluten-free, mild or hot Indian curry paste (such as Patak's)

One 14.5-ounce can unsweetened coconut milk, shaken well

One 15-ounce can chickpeas, rinsed and drained

1 cup frozen peas

Heat the oil in a large, deep skillet or Dutch oven with a lid over medium-high heat. Add the butternut squash and potato cubes and sauté just until they start to brown a little, 3 to 4 minutes.

Add the onion, cauliflower, and curry paste, starting with a little and continuing to add until you reach the desired heat level. Cook, stirring constantly for 1 to 2 minutes, or until the paste is combined and the onion is just starting to soften. Add the coconut milk and stir to combine. Cover the pot, lower the heat, and simmer for 15 minutes, or until the vegetables are tender. Add the chickpeas and frozen peas and heat through, 1 to 2 minutes. If adding cooked chicken or meat to the curry, add it with the chickpeas and frozen peas.

Spiced Basmati Rice with Cashews

2 tablespoons olive or grapeseed oil

1/2 teaspoon ground cumin

1/4 teaspoon ground cardamom

1 1/2 cups basmati rice

1 1/2 teaspoons kosher or fine sea salt

2 1/2 cups water

1/2 cup cashews

Heat the oil in a large saucepan. Add the ground cumin and cardamom and cook, stirring, for 1 minute. Add the rice and toast until lightly browned, 3 to 4 minutes. Add the salt and water and bring to a boil. Cover the pan, lower the heat, and simmer until all the water has been absorbed by the rice, about 15 minutes. Let stand for 5 minutes off the heat. Add the cashews and fluff the rice with a fork.

Dairy-Free Mango Lassis

3 heaping cups frozen mango chunks (one and one-half 16-ounce bags)	Juice of 1 large lemon
	3 cups coconut milk
	¼ cup honey (or to taste)

Combine all the ingredients in a high-powered blender or a food processor and process until fully blended and smooth. You may have to scrape down the sides of the blender jar or food processor bowl a couple of times. Serve immediately in glasses with a spoon and straw.

Cottage Comfort

ᘓᘓᘓᘓᘓᘓᘓᘓᘓ

• Dairy-Free
Adaptable

MENU

Shepherd's Pie

Spinach Salad with Mushrooms, Red Onions, and Cranberries

Quick "Baked" Apples

ᘓᘓᘓᘓᘓᘓᘓᘓᘓ

I have fond memories of eating Shepherd's Pie (also known as cottage pie) as a child. My mother usually made it with leftover beef or lamb and potatoes but personally, I love it too much to rely on having leftovers. My mother's baked apples were delicious but took an hour to bake; this is a much quicker version that is equally delicious.

Quick-Cook Strategy

• Start by boiling the potatoes for the mashed potato crust. To save time in peeling, buy the biggest Yukon Gold potatoes you can find; it is quicker to peel 6 potatoes rather than 12. Peel the carrots at the same time. Cutting the potatoes into small pieces will help them cook faster. Cook the potatoes in a large pan to help speed it along, and make sure you cover the pan while cooking; this keeps the heat in the pan where you need it.

Serves 6

- Chop the vegetables for the meat filling in ¼-inch pieces; this will help them brown and cook faster. Use a large skillet.
- Get help where you can and buy prewashed spinach and presliced mushrooms; they are slightly more expensive but a huge time-saver.
- Instead of using half a small red onion for the salad and 1 medium onion for the Shepherd's Pie, use 1 large red onion, thinly slice a quarter of it for the salad, and chop the rest for the Shepherd's Pie.
- Get the skillet for the Shepherd's Pie hot and add the vegetables as you chop them. If you add the ingredients in the order listed in the recipe, everything will cook perfectly.
- While I love the flavor of the white cheddar in this recipe, I have yet to be able to buy it preshredded. If you are really short on time, use preshredded sharp cheddar instead. The cheese can be omitted completely for a dairy-free version.

Shepherd's Pie

MASHED POTATO CRUST

3 pounds Yukon Gold potatoes, peeled and cut into ½-inch pieces

3 tablespoons unsalted butter or dairy-free butter substitute

¼ cup milk (dairy-free is fine)

1 cup white cheddar cheese, grated on the large holes of a box grater (omit for dairy-free)

Kosher or fine sea salt

Freshly ground black pepper

MEAT FILLING

2 tablespoons olive oil

2 carrots, cut into ¼-inch dice

1 medium onion, cut into ¼-inch dice

2 garlic cloves, minced

1 teaspoon kosher or fine sea salt

½ teaspoon freshly ground black pepper

1 tablespoon tomato paste

1½ pounds ground sirloin

½ cup gluten-free beef stock

1 tablespoon Worcestershire sauce

3 to 4 dashes hot sauce (optional)

1 cup frozen peas

Prepare the mashed potato crust. Bring a large, covered pot of salted water to a boil. Add the chopped potatoes, cover, and boil until tender, 15 to 20 minutes. Drain and return the potatoes to the hot pot and return to the stovetop. Mash the potatoes with a potato masher or a handheld mixer. When there is no more steam coming from the potatoes, turn off the heat. Add the butter, milk, and cheese, if using, and mix well. Season with salt and pepper to taste. Set aside.

Prepare the meat filling. Heat a large skillet over medium-high heat. Add the olive oil, then the carrots, onions, garlic, salt, and pepper. Cook, stirring often, until the vegetables begin to brown and soften, about 5 minutes. Add the tomato paste and mix well. Add the ground sirloin, breaking it up with a spatula into small pieces, and cook until the meat is no longer pink, about 10 minutes. Add

the beef stock, Worcestershire sauce, and hot sauce, increase the heat to high, and cook for about 5 minutes, or until most of the liquid has evaporated. Stir in the frozen peas. Taste and add additional salt and pepper, if desired.

Preheat the broiler.

Transfer the meat filling to an ovenproof 1½-quart baking dish and spread it out evenly. Place the mashed potato mixture on top and spread it out to the edges of the dish, smoothing the top. Rake the potatoes with a fork first lengthwise and then crosswise to create little peaks. Place the pie under the broiler for 5 to 6 minutes, or until the mashed potato crust is nicely browned.

Spinach Salad with Mushrooms, Red Onions, and Cranberries

2 tablespoons red wine vinegar

1 tablespoon honey

½ teaspoon kosher or fine sea salt

¼ teaspoon freshly ground black pepper

6 tablespoons extra-virgin olive oil

⅓ cup dried cranberries

4 ounces sliced white mushrooms

¼ small red onion, thinly sliced

6 ounces prewashed baby spinach

In the bottom of a salad bowl, combine the vinegar, honey, salt, and pepper with a whisk. Add the olive oil slowly while whisking. Add the cranberries, mushrooms, and onion slices, stir to coat, and set aside until ready to serve. Just before serving, add the spinach and toss. Taste and add additional salt and pepper, if needed.

Quick "Baked" Apples

3 large tart apples (such as
  Granny Smith)
3 tablespoons unsalted butter
or dairy-free butter substitute

6 tablespoons brown sugar
$1/4$ cup dried cranberries
$1/4$ cup chopped walnuts

Cut the apples in half and remove the core with a spoon or knife to make a well in the center of each apple about 1 inch wide. Place the apples in a microwave-safe baking dish. Add $1/2$ tablespoon of butter to the center of each apple half. Divide the brown sugar and dried cranberries among the apples. Cover the dish with plastic wrap and microwave on high power for $3 1/2$ minutes. Test the apples by piercing them with a knife; they should be soft but not mushy. If too firm, microwave for another minute or two. Let cool for a couple minutes, covered, before serving. Top with chopped walnuts and serve.

Asian Ragu

• Dairy-Free

MENU

Asian Noodles and Meat Sauce

Thai Carrot and Cucumber Salad

Quick Mango Sticky Rice

This is an Asian take on spaghetti and Bolognese sauce. Instead of pasta, rice sticks (Asian rice noodles) are used and the meat sauce is made with ground pork and is full of Asian flavors such as ginger and red curry sauce.

Mango sticky rice is a delicious dessert served in Thai restaurants. Using the microwave to prepare the rice and frozen mango chunks saves tons of time with no sacrifice of flavor.

Quick-Cook Strategy

- Get the sticky rice and rice sticks soaking first. If they soak a little longer it is fine—better they wait for you than you wait for them.
- If you have a mini food processor this is a great time to use it. You can toss in the shallots, garlic, and ginger for the meat sauce and chop it all up at the same time. If you don't have shallots, use a medium red onion instead.

Serves 4

- Prepare the meat sauce in a large skillet; it will cook faster and give you the room to toss in the rice sticks at the end.
- Preshredded carrots are a huge time-saver; look for matchstick cut. Make the dressing for the salad and add the carrots and cucumbers while the meat sauce is cooking. If the dressing sits for a little, it gets better.
- If you have leftover mango sticky rice, serve it for breakfast. Just reheat it for a few minutes in the microwave.

Tapas Party, page 110

Asian Ragu, page 83

Spring Fling, page 94

Quick
Comfort, page 62

Banana-Date Muffins, page 164

Piña Colada Smoothie, page 161

Breakfast Quesadilla, page 162

Whole Grain Overnight Porridge, page 163

Quick Roasted Beet Salad, page 174

Brined Pork Chops, with Spicy Pear Chutney, page 190

Date Night, page 118

Whole Grain Pancake
and Biscuit Mix, page 24

Wine- and Rosemary-Braised Lamb Shanks
with White Bean Mash, page 195

Pistachio-Cranberry-Goat Cheese–
Stuffed Pork Tenderloin, page 127

Oven-Fried Chicken, page 139

Chocolate-Strawberry Fool, page 124

Polenta Potpies, page 69

Spicy Noodles, page 189

Cookies and Cream No-Bake Cheese-cakes, page 143

Almost Instant Nutella
Mousse, page 130

All-American Meat
Loaf Dinner, page 33

Quick Thanksgiving, page 144

Asian Noodles and Meat Sauce

8 ounces rice sticks or rice vermicelli	1 pound lean ground pork
2 tablespoons grapeseed or olive oil	3/4 cup gluten-free chicken stock
4 large shallots, diced	1 tablespoon fish sauce
4 large garlic cloves, minced	1 tablespoon gluten-free soy sauce
One 2-inch piece fresh ginger, peeled and minced	2 teaspoons light brown sugar
2 teaspoons gluten-free red curry paste	1/2 cup fresh basil leaves, torn
	1/2 cup fresh mint leaves, torn
	1/4 cup dry roasted peanuts, chopped

Soak the rice sticks in hot water until tender, 5 to 6 minutes, or according to the package directions. Drain and rinse under cold running water. Set aside.

Heat the oil in a large skillet over medium-high heat. Add the shallots, garlic, and ginger and sauté until the shallots are tender, about 4 minutes. Add the curry paste and stir to combine. Add the ground pork and break it up with a spoon or spatula. Cook until browned, about 5 minutes. Whisk together the chicken stock, fish sauce, soy sauce, and brown sugar and add to the meat. Cook until the liquid has reduced by half, about 5 minutes. Add the noodles and toss to coat with the sauce. Transfer to a serving dish and top with the torn basil and mint and the chopped peanuts.

Thai Carrot and Cucumber Salad

2 tablespoons fish sauce
2 tablespoons freshly squeezed
   lime juice
1 tablespoon sugar

Pinch crushed red pepper flakes
2 cups shredded carrots
1 hothouse cucumber, peeled and
   thinly sliced

In a medium mixing bowl, whisk together the fish sauce, lime juice, sugar, and red pepper flakes. Add the carrots and cucumbers and toss to coat.

Quick Mango Sticky Rice

1 cup sticky rice (also called sushi rice, sweet rice, or glutinous rice)

One 13.5-ounce can unsweetened coconut milk, shaken well

¼ cup firmly packed light brown sugar

¼ teaspoon kosher or fine sea salt

2 teaspoons cornstarch or tapioca starch

2 tablespoons water

1 teaspoon pure vanilla extract

One 16-ounce bag frozen mango chunks, thawed

Fresh mint sprigs for garnish (optional)

Place the rice in a microwave-safe bowl, cover with 1 inch of warm water, and set aside for 10 minutes.

Cover the bowl with plastic wrap and microwave on high for 3 minutes. Carefully remove the plastic wrap, stir, re-cover, and microwave for another 3 minutes. Continue cooking and stirring in 3-minute intervals until the rice has absorbed the water and is tender, about 9 minutes depending on the wattage of your microwave oven.

While the rice is cooking, prepare the sauce. In a large saucepan, heat the coconut milk, brown sugar, and salt until it just starts to boil. Mix the cornstarch with the water and stir into the coconut milk mixture. Cook, stirring, for about 1 minute, or until the mixture starts to thicken. Lower the heat and stir in the vanilla, then add the cooked rice and mango. Heat gently for 2 to 3 minutes, or until the rice has absorbed some of the coconut milk mixture and the mango pieces are heated through. Serve warm, garnished with sprigs of mint, if desired.

- Vegetarian

- Dairy-Free
Adaptable

Middle Eastern Dinner

ᵒ᷈ᵒ᷈ᵒ᷈ᵒ᷈ᵒ᷈ᵒ᷈ᵒ᷈

MENU

Falafel Burgers

Creamy Tahini Sauce

Quinoa Tabbouleh

Honey-Roasted Plums

ᵒ᷈ᵒ᷈ᵒ᷈ᵒ᷈ᵒ᷈ᵒ᷈ᵒ᷈

This is a simple vegetarian dinner that meat eaters will love as well. A falafel burger is topped with a creamy tahini sauce and served with a gluten-free version of the classic Middle Eastern salad tabbouleh. Tabbouleh is traditionally made with cracked wheat, but in this recipe the wheat is replaced with quinoa.

It may seem like there is more Creamy Tahini Sauce than you will need for this menu, but in my family we like a high sauce-to-falafel ratio, and I bet you'll find yourself in a similar position. In the unlikely event you have left-over sauce, save it; it is delicious as a dip with pieces of raw vegetables such as cucumber or carrots.

Quick-Cook Strategy

- Start the quinoa boiling first thing; it has to simmer for about 15 minutes, which creates a pocket of time for you to get most everything else done. Using prerinsed quinoa saves time and effort.
- As soon as the quinoa is started, move on to the plums; they need to roast in the oven for about 25 minutes. Remove from the oven before starting to eat and they will cool in time for dessert. If topping with mascarpone cheese, add this just before serving. Chop the pistachios ahead and have them waiting.
- Cook the quinoa in a large pot, such as a Dutch oven or spaghetti pot, which will allow the water to boil faster and the quinoa to cook faster.
- Chop the parsley for both the burgers and the tabbouleh at the same time.
- Squeeze all the fresh lemon juice you will need at one time. Microwaving lemons for about 10 seconds before juicing will yield more juice. For this entire meal you will need 2 to 3 average-size lemons.

Falafel Burgers

Two 15.5-ounce cans chickpeas, rinsed and drained	½ teaspoon freshly ground black pepper
1 bunch scallions (6 to 8), trimmed and roughly chopped	6 tablespoons chickpea flour, Sweet Rice Flour Blend (page 17), or any all-purpose gluten-free flour
1 small bunch flat-leaf parsley (about 1 cup), roughly chopped	¼ cup olive oil
2 teaspoons ground cumin	8 whole lettuce leaves
½ teaspoon garlic powder	Creamy Tahini Sauce (page 91)
1 teaspoon kosher or fine sea salt	Chili garlic sauce (optional)

Put the chickpeas, scallions, parsley, cumin, garlic powder, salt, pepper, and 2 tablespoons flour in a food processor fitted with the steel blade. Process until the mixture turns into a coarse paste. Divide the mixture into four equal portions and shape into patties. Put the remaining flour onto a plate and lightly coat the patties with flour.

Heat the olive oil in a large skillet over medium-high heat. Add the patties and cook for 2 to 3 minutes per side or until crispy.

To serve, place 2 lettuce leaves on each plate and top with a falafel burger. Top with a little Creamy Tahini Sauce and offer the rest on the side. If you like dishes with some heat, add a dab of chili garlic sauce on top of the tahini sauce.

Creamy Tahini Sauce

½ cup sesame tahini

½ cup plain Greek yogurt, fat-free or lowfat (to make dairy-free omit and substitute with another ½ cup sesame tahini)

¼ cup freshly squeezed lemon juice

1 garlic clove, minced

½ to ¾ teaspoon kosher or fine sea salt

½ to ¾ cup water

Place the sesame tahini, yogurt, if using, lemon juice, garlic, ½ teaspoon of salt, and ½ cup of water in a blender. Blend until smooth and thick; it should be the consistency of lightly whipped cream. Add a little more water, if necessary. Taste and add more salt, if needed. Transfer to small serving bowl. Leftover sauce can be covered and stored in the refrigerator.

Quinoa Tabbouleh

2 cups water
1 cup prerinsed quinoa
$\frac{1}{4}$ cup olive oil
$\frac{1}{2}$ teaspoon kosher or fine sea salt
$\frac{1}{2}$ teaspoon freshly ground black
    pepper

$\frac{1}{4}$ cup freshly squeezed lemon
    juice
2 tomatoes, finely chopped
1 hothouse cucumber, finely diced
1 cup flat-leaf parsley, finely
    chopped

In a large saucepan, combine the water and quinoa and bring to a boil over high heat. Cover the pan, reduce the heat to medium-low, and simmer until all the water is absorbed, about 15 minutes. Remove from the heat and set aside, covered, for 5 minutes.

While the quinoa is simmering, combine the rest of the ingredients and set aside until the quinoa has finished cooking. Fluff the quinoa with a fork, add the vegetable mixture, and stir gently to combine. Taste and add a little more salt and pepper, if needed. Serve at room temperature.

The salad can be made ahead and stored, covered, in the refrigerator. Allow to come to room temperature before serving.

Honey-Roasted Plums

½ cup honey

1 tablespoon unsalted butter or
    nondairy butter substitute

2 teaspoons freshly squeezed
    lemon juice

4 large, firm but ripe red or black
    plums, halved and pitted

¼ cup mascarpone cheese, at
    room temperature (optional;
    omit for dairy-free)

¼ cup chopped pistachios

Preheat the oven to 400 degrees.

In a small saucepan, melt the honey and butter with the lemon juice over medium-low heat. Pour half the honey syrup into an 8-inch square baking dish, add the halved plums, and toss to coat thoroughly. Arrange the plums in the baking dish, cut side down.

Roast the plums for 15 minutes, or until barely tender and beginning to brown on the bottom. Turn the plums and spoon the remaining honey syrup over them. Roast the plums for 10 minutes more, or until tender but not falling apart. Let cool slightly.

To serve, transfer the plums to individual serving plates and drizzle with the honey syrup. Top with a dollop of mascarpone, if using, sprinkle with the chopped pistachios, and serve.

• Dairy-Free
Adaptable

Spring Fling

MENU

Potato- and Herb-Crusted Cod

Skillet Potatoes

Smashed Minty Peas

Balsamic Strawberries with Mascarpone Cream

Whenever I buy instant mashed potatoes from the store, I try to hide them at the bottom of my cart, horrified someone might see them. While I would never in a million years actually use them to make mashed potatoes, they do have their uses in gluten-free cooking. One is making a crunchy, herb-specked crust for fish fillets. It transforms a regular piece of baked fish into a crispy work of art, all the flavor of those fancy restaurant potato-crusted fish dishes without all the work. I serve this on a bed of crispy skillet potatoes with a side of minty smashed peas, and each bite is like a little taste of spring.

You may think that vinegar and strawberries is an odd combination, but trust me, they were made for each other. Topped with a dollop of whipped mascarpone cheese, this dessert is simple but elegant. If you are dairy-free, try a little scoop of dairy-free ice cream instead of the mascarpone cream, or just forgo any accompaniment altogether; the strawberries and balsamic are certainly dessert-worthy all on their own.

Quick-Cook Strategy

- As always when cooking a meal that requires the oven, preheat it first thing.
- Slice the strawberries and let them macerate in the sugar while preparing the rest of the meal.
- I prepare the fish, fry the crispy side, and lay the fillets on a baking sheet ready to go into the oven. Then I wipe out the skillet and use it again to fry the potatoes. Not only does it save time but more importantly, it also means one less pan to wash. I put the fish into the oven about 10 minutes before I am ready to serve dinner.
- Frozen peas are not only a huge time-saver, they are often better quality than the peas you can get in the store as they are flash frozen just after picking. Putting a lid on the pan when boiling the water for the peas will help it boil faster. I bring the water to a boil, then add the frozen peas and only cook them for about 2 minutes, which keeps them bright green and prevents that mushy pea texture that comes from overcooking peas.
- While the potatoes are frying, the fish is in the oven, and the water is boiling for the peas, you will have a little pocket of time to prepare the mascarpone cream, if using. Whip it and keep in the refrigerator until time for dessert.

Potato- and Herb-Crusted Cod

½ (heaping) cup of instant potato flakes

½ teaspoon kosher or fine sea salt, plus more for seasoning the fish

½ teaspoon freshly ground black pepper, plus more for seasoning the fish

½ bunch chives, minced

4 lemons

2 tablespoons Dijon mustard

Four 6-ounce fillets of cod (halibut also works well)

2 tablespoons olive or grapeseed oil

Preheat the oven to 400 degrees. Spray a rimmed baking sheet with gluten-free, nonstick cooking spray and set aside.

On a dinner plate, combine the potato flakes with ½ teaspoon salt, ½ teaspoon pepper, and the minced chives.

Quarter the lemons. Put the Dijon mustard into a small bowl, squeeze a few drops of lemon juice from one of the lemon quarters into it, and mix. Place the lemon quarters on the prepared baking sheet. Sprinkle a little salt and pepper on both sides of the fish fillets and then brush the Dijon mixture on one side of each fillet. Dip the coated side of the fish into the potato flake mixture and press down so the mixture adheres to the fish.

Heat the oil in a large skillet over medium-high heat until very hot but not smoking. Fry the fish, coated side down, in the hot oil until browned and crispy, about 1 minute. Do not overcrowd the pan while frying. If you need to, fry the fish in batches. Lay the fish fillets, crispy side up, on the prepared baking sheet with the lemon quarters and bake until the fish is cooked through and just starts to flake, 7 to 8 minutes.

Serve the fish with the heated lemon quarters.

Skillet Potatoes

2 pounds baby Yukon Gold potatoes	1 teaspoon kosher or fine sea salt
2 tablespoons olive or grapeseed oil	½ teaspoon freshly ground black pepper

Wash the potatoes and cut them into ¼-inch slices. Heat the oil in a large skillet over medium-high heat and add the potatoes. Season the potatoes with the salt and pepper. Toss the potatoes in the hot oil, then spread them into an even layer in the pan and let them fry for a few minutes, undisturbed, until they start to brown. Then turn the potatoes occasionally to brown them on both sides and cook them through evenly. Fry until tender yet crispy, about 15 minutes. If the potatoes are browning too fast, lower the heat.

If serving with the cod, place a layer of fried potatoes on each dinner plate, then top with a fillet of cooked cod.

Smashed Minty Peas

2 garlic cloves, smashed and peeled

1 teaspoon kosher or fine sea salt

1 pound frozen peas

2 tablespoons olive oil (more if making dairy-free)

$\frac{1}{4}$ cup fresh mint leaves

$\frac{1}{2}$ teaspoon freshly ground black pepper

2 tablespoons heavy cream (optional; omit for dairy-free)

Put the garlic cloves into a medium saucepan and fill to three-quarters with water. Cover the pan and bring to a boil over high heat. Once the water is boiling, remove the lid, add the salt and the peas, and boil just until the peas are heated and tender, about 2 minutes. Drain the water and put the peas and garlic cloves into a food processor. Add the olive oil, mint leaves, and pepper and pulse a few times until blended but still a little chunky. Add the cream, if using, and pulse a couple more times. If you are not using the cream, you may want to add another tablespoon or two of olive oil to give it a creamy texture. If you don't have a food processor, simply mash the peas and garlic with the olive oil, pepper, and cream, if using, mince the mint, and stir it in. Taste and season with a little more salt if needed. Return the smashed peas to the hot pot to keep them warm until serving time.

Balsamic Strawberries with Mascarpone Cream

2 pints fresh strawberries

2 teaspoons plus 2 tablespoons sugar

¼ cup balsamic vinegar

1 lemon, zested and juiced

1 tiny pinch freshly ground black pepper

½ cup mascarpone cheese

¼ cup heavy whipping cream

Wash and hull the strawberries and cut them in half lengthwise. Place them in a bowl, sprinkle with 2 teaspoons of the sugar, mix, and set aside.

In a small saucepan, combine the balsamic vinegar with the remaining 2 tablespoons of sugar, the juice of the lemon, and the black pepper. Cook over high heat until the mixture reduces by half and thickens slightly, 2 to 3 minutes. Let the mixture cool slightly, then pour over the strawberries and toss to combine.

Whisk the mascarpone cheese with the lemon zest and heavy cream, using a handheld mixer or a whisk, until creamy and smooth.

To serve, divide the strawberries and the juices among four pretty goblets or dessert bowls and top with a dollop of the mascarpone cream.

Easy Entertaining

SOMETIMES WE ENTERTAIN because we want to, and sometimes we entertain because we feel obliged to do so. Regardless of the circumstances, there is no reason for the host or hostess to feel overwhelmed and to spend hours in the kitchen cooking only to become too exhausted to enjoy the party.

In a perfect world we would have plenty of time to decorate, prepare food, and then relax in a nice bubble bath before a party or dinner. Unfortunately, life is never as perfect as we would like.

The first time I ever officially entertained as a young bride, I made every mistake possible; my menu was too complicated, with lots of last-minute preparation, I had fussy, time-consuming decorations, and I didn't leave myself enough time to get everything ready. I was too stressed out to actually enjoy my guests, spent the whole evening running back and forth from the kitchen to the dining room, and all I could think was that I could not wait for the evening to be over.

Since then I have learned a thing or two. If time permits, I get as much done beforehand as possible: I set the table the night before, make dishes ahead, and I have learned to keep it simple. Instead of making a bunch of complicated dishes, I focus on one that really shines and I take help where I can get it, with items like prewashed salad greens and precut vegetables.

Decorations need not be complicated; a simple vase of flowers or lovely bowl of fruit can be elegant and beautiful.

Often the gluten intolerant feel they cannot serve the same food to their guests as they eat and are compelled to introduce gluten-filled food they normally would not have in the house. Not only is this dangerous because of cross contamination but it is also completely unnecessary. As long as your food tastes good, no one will miss the gluten.

In this chapter, I offer menus for entertaining that can be prepared in an hour or less. If you have time to break up the preparations and do some of the menu ahead of time, then by all means do so.

Client Dinner

MENU

Almond-Crusted Chicken Piccata

Quinoa Pilaf

Arugula Salad

Blueberry Fool

As much as I love my husband, he does have a habit of springing things on me at the last minute. Impromptu jaunts to New York are very much appreciated by me; last-minute dinner parties for very important clients, not so much.

This dinner party was born with a phone call from said husband stating that he had just been bragging to his clients about what a wonderful cook I was. So they decided to have dinner at our house instead of a fancy restaurant and he would be home, guests in tow, in an hour. The first fifteen minutes of that hour I spent stashing clutter in the closets and running a dust rag (or in this case his favorite shirt) over every surface. The last forty-five were spent making this simple dinner, elegant enough for even the most important of clients.

Serves 4

Quick-Cook Strategy

- Prep all your vegetables and herbs at one time like they do in restaurants. Chopped parsley is used in both the Chicken Piccata and the Quinoa Pilaf; chop the amount you need for both at one time.
- Squeeze enough lemon juice for both the Chicken Piccata and the Arugula Salad at one time.
- Sliced almonds are used in the Quinoa Pilaf and are quicker to grind for the Chicken Piccata; no need to buy two different kinds of almonds.
- Start the Quinoa Pilaf first as it takes the longest, then get started on the Chicken Piccata. Make the Arugula Salad and Blueberry Fool while the chicken breasts are cooking.
- Bags of prewashed baby arugula speed up the salad-making process.

Almond-Crusted Chicken Piccata

4 boneless, skinless chicken breast halves, 6 ounces each

1 cup raw almonds (or you can use ground almond meal)

¼ cup grated Parmesan cheese

1 teaspoon kosher or sea salt

½ teaspoon freshly ground black pepper

¼ cup olive oil

4 tablespoons (½ stick) unsalted butter

½ cup gluten-free chicken stock or dry white wine

3 tablespoons freshly squeezed lemon juice

¼ cup capers packed in brine, drained

¼ cup chopped flat-leaf parsley

Additional lemons for garnish and serving

Lay a piece of plastic wrap on a work surface, place a chicken breast half on top, and lay another piece of plastic wrap on top. Pound the chicken breast with a meat mallet, rolling pin, or the bottom of a heavy skillet until it is about ¼ inch thick. Repeat with the remaining chicken breasts.

Put almonds into the bowl of a food processor and process, in pulses, until the almonds turn into a fine meal. Be careful not to overprocess and turn them into paste. Add the Parmesan cheese, salt, and pepper and pulse a couple more times to mix. If using almond meal, just mix the meal, cheese, salt, and pepper together. Spread the mixture on a large plate.

Rinse the pounded chicken breasts in water and shake off the excess. Dredge the chicken in the almond mixture, gently pressing the mixture onto the chicken.

Heat a large skillet over medium-high heat. Add the olive oil and 2 table-spoons of the butter. Once the oil is hot and the butter has melted, place one or two of the dredged chicken breasts in the pan—do not overcrowd! Cook for 3 to 4 minutes, or until they are well browned. Turn and cook for 3 to 4 minutes on the other side. Transfer the cooked chicken breasts to a serving dish and

cover with aluminum foil to keep them warm. You can also put the plate in a warm oven. Repeat the procedure with the remaining chicken breasts.

Add the wine or chicken stock and lemon juice to the skillet. Scrape the bottom of the skillet to release all the browned bits of almond. Add the capers and cook until the sauce has reduced by about half; it should be the consistency of light syrup. Stir in the remaining butter until melted.

Pour the sauce over the chicken breasts, top with chopped parsley, and serve with lemon slices or wedges.

Quinoa Pilaf

3 teaspoons olive oil
½ cup finely minced white or
    yellow onion (about ½
    medium onion)
1 cup prerinsed quinoa
1 garlic clove, finely minced
1½ cups water

1 teaspoon kosher or sea salt
¼ cup slivered almonds
1 scallion, white and green parts
    finely minced
¼ cup finely minced flat-leaf
    parsley
Freshly ground black pepper

Heat 1 teaspoon of the olive oil in a large saucepan over medium heat. Add the minced white or yellow onion and cook for about 2 minutes, or until the onion is translucent. Add the quinoa and garlic and cook for about 3 minutes; you want the quinoa to lightly toast, but you do not want the garlic to brown. Add the water and salt. Increase the heat, bring to a full boil, cover, then reduce the heat to medium-low. Simmer for about 15 minutes, or until all the liquid is absorbed and the quinoa is tender.

While the quinoa is simmering, toast the almond slivers in a dry skillet over high heat until they are lightly browned and fragrant, stirring often. Watch them carefully so they do not burn. Remove from the heat and set aside.

When the quinoa is done, remove from the heat and let sit in the pan, covered, for about 3 minutes. Transfer to a serving bowl and fluff with a fork. Add the scallion, parsley, and almonds. Drizzle with the remaining 2 teaspoons of olive oil and toss to combine. Taste and add salt and pepper, if needed.

Arugula Salad

12 ounces baby arugula, washed
  and dried
¼ cup extra-virgin olive oil
2 tablespoons freshly squeezed
  lemon juice

Kosher or fine sea salt
Freshly ground black pepper
1 ounce Parmesan cheese,
  shaved with a vegetable
  peeler

Place the arugula in a salad bowl. Toss with the olive oil and lemon juice and season to taste with salt and pepper. Shave the Parmesan on top and serve.

Blueberry Fool

2 cups fresh or frozen (slightly
   thawed) blueberries
2 to 3 tablespoons agave nectar
   (or sugar) depending on the
   berry sweetness

1¼ cup heavy whipping cream

Reserve four berries for garnish and place the remaining berries along with the agave (or sugar) in a blender or food processor. Puree until smooth.

Whip the cream until stiff peaks form. Reserve some of the whipped cream for garnish and fold the puree into the remaining cream until almost all the streaks are gone. Spoon the Blueberry Fool into 4 pretty goblets. Garnish with the reserved cream and berries. Serve immediately, or refrigerate for up to an hour or so.

Tapas Party

ᑫᑫᑫᑫᑫᑫᑫᑫᑫᑫ

MENU

Sangaritas

Spanish Tortilla

Glazed Chorizo Bites

Manchego-Stuffed Peppers

Roasted Shrimp with Romesco Dip

Mini Almond Orange Cakes

ᑫᑫᑫᑫᑫᑫᑫᑫᑫᑫ

Cocktail parties are my favorite way to entertain. People mingle and get to know each other, there is no setting the table, and the atmosphere is relaxed and easy, allowing me to enjoy my own party. This tapas party is by far my favorite cocktail party theme.

To keep things simple, instead of stocking a full bar I like to make one cocktail for the evening, in this case Sangaritas—a sangria with tequila-soaked fruit. Add sparkling and still water, and a bottle or two of red wine to round out the bar. For a nonalcoholic "mocktail," mix the juice from the zested oranges used in the Mini Almond Orange Cakes with sparkling water and ice. The sangarita just gets better and better as it sits, so if you have time, make it

the night before. I like to use Malbec, a red wine from Argentina, in my sangarita; it is just as delicious as Spanish wine but less expensive.

If you have more than ten people coming over, you can easily add platters of Spanish cured meats from the deli counter, Spanish almonds and olives, and a nice chunk of Manchego cheese with some fruit to fill out your cocktail party buffet.

I always serve something a little sweet at cocktail parties and think it fitting to make it in miniature form to go along with the whole finger food aspect of cocktail parties. If you prefer, you can bake the Mini Almond Orange Cakes as one large cake; just pour the batter into a well-greased, 8-inch cake pan and bake for 30 to 35 minutes.

Quick-Cook Strategy

- Start by preheating the oven to 375 degrees for the mini cakes. Once they are done, increase the oven temperature to 400 degrees. Once the peppers and shrimp are done, turn on the broiler.
- Get the sangarita mix started, and while the fruit is soaking up the tequila, prepare and bake the mini cakes.
- A microplane grater makes fast work of zesting the oranges for the mini cakes.
- Prepare the Romesco Dip in the food processor first and then you don't even have to wash it out to make the Manchego-Stuffed Peppers.

Sangaritas

2 bottles red wine, such as Malbec	¼ cup agave nectar (or sugar)
2 lemons, washed and cut into wedges	½ cup tequila
2 oranges, washed and cut into wedges	Club soda (about 8 ounces)

Place the red wine in the freezer to chill it while preparing the fruit. Combine the lemon and orange wedges with the agave (or sugar) in a bowl. Press the fruit gently to expel some of the juices. Pour in the tequila and let macerate for 15 minutes.

Pour the wine into a large pitcher, add the fruit along with the tequila, and stir to combine. Refrigerate until serving time. The sangarita mix can be made up to 2 days ahead. To serve, pour into wineglasses and finish each with a splash of club soda.

Spanish Tortilla

¼ cup olive oil	2 teaspoons kosher or fine sea salt
2 garlic cloves, peeled and smashed slightly	1 teaspoon freshly ground black pepper
3 to 4 sprigs fresh thyme	1 small red onion, thinly sliced
1½ pounds baby Yukon Gold potatoes, sliced about ¼ inch thick	12 large eggs, lightly beaten

Preheat the broiler.

Heat the olive oil in a 12-inch ovenproof skillet over medium heat. Add the garlic cloves and thyme sprigs and cook for about a minute to infuse the oil with their flavors. Remove and discard the garlic cloves and thyme sprigs. Add the potatoes, salt, and pepper to the oil in the skillet and cook for about 10 minutes, stirring occasionally. You want to cook the potatoes through without browning them too much; a little color is fine. If the potatoes are browning too fast, reduce the heat. Add the sliced onion and cook for another 5 to 10 minutes, or until the onion is soft and beginning to brown and the potatoes are fork-tender. Reduce the heat to low.

Pour in the beaten eggs and gently pull the edges of the egg mixture to the center as it cooks so that any uncooked eggs run underneath. Once the eggs are set around the edges and the mixture looks mostly cooked, place the skillet under the broiler for 2 to 3 minutes, or until the eggs are fully set, golden, and slightly puffed.

Run a dinner knife around the edge of the tortilla to loosen it and slide it onto a serving platter or cutting board. The tortilla can be served warm or at room temperature. Cut into wedges to serve.

Glazed Chorizo Bites

2 tablespoons olive oil

2 pounds cured chorizo (the type you slice, not crumble) cut into 1-inch chunks

¼ cup balsamic or sherry vinegar

2 tablespoons honey

Heat the olive oil in a large skillet over medium heat. Add the chorizo and cook until the edges start to brown and the chorizo is heated through, 4 to 5 minutes, stirring occasionally to ensure even browning. Drain off excess fat. Add the vinegar and honey to the skillet, increase the heat to high, and cook, stirring, until the liquid becomes thick and syrupy, 3 or 4 minutes. Transfer to a serving dish. Serve warm or at room temperature.

Manchego-Stuffed Peppers

Two 12-ounce jars whole roasted
   red peppers
1/2 bunch fresh thyme
8 ounces Manchego cheese
1 cup blanched, slivered almonds
2 tablespoons balsamic or sherry
   vinegar

1/2 teaspoon kosher or fine sea
   salt
1/2 teaspoon freshly ground black
   pepper
Olive oil for drizzling

Preheat the oven to 400 degrees.

Drain the peppers and pat them dry with paper towels. Cut each pepper in half lengthwise and set aside. Set half the thyme sprigs aside.

Cut the rind off the cheese, cut the cheese into chunks, and put in a food processor fitted with the steel blade. Pull the leaves off the remaining thyme sprigs and add to the food processor along with the almonds, vinegar, salt, and pepper. Process until the mixture resembles a coarse meal. Measure and reserve about 1/4 cup of the mixture. Spoon some of the mixture onto each red pepper half and roll up the pepper. Place seam side down in a 9 × 12-inch baking dish. Repeat with the remaining peppers. Top the peppers with the reserved cheese-almond mixture and the reserved thyme sprigs. Drizzle with olive oil. Bake for 8 to 10 minutes, or until heated through and the topping is nicely browned. Serve hot, warm, or at room temperature.

Roasted Shrimp with Romesco Dip

2 pounds fresh or frozen, thawed, large shrimp, peeled and deveined, tails intact
Kosher or fine sea salt
Freshly ground black pepper
Juice of 1 lemon
3 to 4 tablespoons olive oil
½ cup blanched, slivered almonds

1 garlic clove, peeled
½ cup jarred roasted red peppers
1 teaspoon smoked, sweet, or hot paprika (use hot if you like spicy)
1 tablespoon balsamic or sherry vinegar

Preheat the oven to 400 degrees.

Place the shrimp in a baking dish and sprinkle with about a teaspoon of both salt and pepper. Add the lemon juice and 1 tablespoon of the olive oil and toss to coat. Roast the shrimp in the oven for 5 to 6 minutes, or until they turn pink and are firm to the touch.

While the shrimp are roasting, make the Romesco Dip. Put the almonds and garlic clove in the bowl of a food processor fitted with the steel blade and pulse to grind. Add the roasted red peppers, paprika, vinegar, and a big pinch of salt and pepper and process until combined. With the machine running, add 2 to 3 tablespoons of the olive oil through the feed tube until the mixture becomes a thick dip. Transfer to a small serving dish. Serve with the roasted shrimp.

Mini Almond Orange Cakes

4 large eggs, separated	1/2 teaspoon kosher or fine sea
1/2 cup sugar	salt
5 teaspoons (packed) finely	1 1/2 cups blanched almond flour
grated orange zest (from 4 to 5	1 to 2 tablespoons confectioners'
average-size oranges)	sugar for dusting

Preheat the oven to 375 degrees. Spray 2 mini muffin tins (24 muffin cups per pan) or one 8-inch cake pan with gluten-free, nonstick cooking spray.

In a medium mixing bowl, beat the egg whites until foamy, starting on low speed and increasing to high. Gradually add 1/4 cup of the sugar and continue to beat until stiff peaks form. Combine the egg yolks with the remaining 4 tablespoons of sugar, the orange zest, and salt in a mixing bowl and beat until thick and smooth, about 2 minutes. Add the almond flour and stir to combine. Fold a large spoonful of the egg whites into the almond mixture. Gently fold in the remaining whites. Divide the mixture among the prepared pan(s) (a small ice cream scoop is useful for this if making individual cakes) and bake for 10 minutes for mini cakes, 30 to 35 minutes for a large cake, or until lightly browned and a toothpick inserted into the center comes out clean. Let cool in the pan(s) for 5 minutes, then transfer to a wire rack to finish cooling.

Place some confectioners' sugar in a small strainer and dust the cake(s) lightly just before serving.

- Dairy-Free Adaptable

- Grain-Free

Date Night

෩෩෩෩෩෩෩෩෩

MENU

Steakhouse Filet Mignon

Roasted Asparagus

Easy Blender Béarnaise Sauce

Chocolate-Strawberry Fool

෩෩෩෩෩෩෩෩෩

I have always felt that going out for dinner with a loved one on Valentine's Day or on an anniversary was far less special than having a romantic dinner for two at home; the waitstaff are intruding, you are surrounded by strangers, and you don't have the choice of music and flowers you would at home. It is also far more expensive.

This menu is, in my opinion, the ultimate date-night dinner but more importantly contains basic methods that can be used in other recipes. The way I cook the filets is the same method I use for any high-quality, expensive, tender beef steaks, only the cooking time may change a little, based on the thickness or size of the cut. It produces beautifully cooked, flavorful steaks every time. If you have ever spent a small fortune on a great steak only to find that once cooked it was overdone on the outside and raw in the center, you will appreciate this.

Roasting any vegetable not only is a great strategy for easy cooking but also brings out the natural sweetness of the vegetables.

Blender béarnaise is something that can be whipped up in a minute or two and adds panache to any meal. Even simple, everyday burger patties and broccoli become a restaurant-quality meal when topped with béarnaise sauce.

I like to round out this meal with some simple mashed potatoes. I slice the steak, place it on top of the potatoes and asparagus, and top the whole thing off with béarnaise.

Strawberries and chocolate are classic romance foods and this easy fool does not disappoint. I wanted to call this dessert "Fool for Love" but thought that just might be too corny. If you don't do dairy, forgo the fool and instead prepare a half recipe of dairy-free chocolate ganache from the All-American Meat Loaf Dinner and dip strawberries into it—*trés romantique.*

Quick-Cook Strategy

- Put an ovenproof grill pan or skillet in the oven and preheat both the oven and the pan at the same time.
- Take the steaks out of the refrigerator and let them sit at room temperature for 10 minutes to take the chill off before cooking.
- If you are going to add mashed potatoes to this menu, get them cut up and boiling before doing anything else.
- Trim and peel the asparagus and set them aside until you take the steaks out of the oven. They will take as long to cook as the steaks take to rest. I always buy the thicker asparagus and peel the bottom half with a vegetable peeler; it takes a tad bit longer to prepare them but they roast faster and most importantly they are far superior—it is amazing how this one little trick can transform asparagus from good to great.

- While the steaks are in the oven, prepare the fool and refrigerate it until serving time.
- Prepare the béarnaise while the asparagus are roasting and the steaks are resting.

Steakhouse Filet Mignon

Two 10-ounce filets
mignons (each about
1½ inches thick)
2 tablespoons olive oil

1 tablespoon kosher or fine sea
salt
1 teaspoon freshly ground black
pepper

Put an ovenproof grill pan or skillet in the oven and preheat to 450 degrees.

Pat the steaks dry with paper towels, then brush them with the olive oil. Combine the salt and pepper on a plate and press the filets into them to coat on both sides.

Once the oven has preheated, carefully remove the hot pan, place it on the stovetop over high heat, add the filets, and sear for 2 minutes without moving them. Turn the filets over and return the skillet to the oven. Cook until an instant-read thermometer (see note) registers 120 degrees for rare, 125 degrees for medium rare, and 130 degrees for medium. Make sure you insert the thermometer sideways into the steak so you reach the center. Medium rare should take 9 to 10 minutes. Remove the skillet from the oven, place a piece of aluminum foil loosely over the filets, and let rest for 10 minutes. Do not skip the resting period as this will allow the juices to redistribute back into the meat and prevent them from pouring out when the steaks are cut.

Note: If you do not have an instant-read thermometer, you can test the steaks using the finger method. Open the palm of your hand and relax your hand. Gently press the tip of your index finger to the tip of your thumb and feel the fleshy area below the thumb with the index finger of your other hand. Notice how that feels—this is what rare beef feels like. To see what medium rare feels like, gently press the tip of your middle finger to the tip of your thumb and feel what the fleshy part below the thumb feels like. For medium, do the same thing using the tip of your ring finger.

Roasted Asparagus

1 pound medium asparagus	¼ teaspoon freshly ground black
1 tablespoon olive oil	pepper
½ teaspoon kosher or fine sea salt	

Preheat the oven to 450 degrees.

Cut the tough woody end off the bottom of the asparagus, usually about 1½ inches. Lightly peel the thicker bottom part of the asparagus stalks with a vegetable peeler. Lay the asparagus spears on a rimmed baking sheet and add the oil, salt, and pepper and toss to coat. Roast for 8 to 10 minutes, or until they are still green but tender.

Easy Blender Béarnaise Sauce

1 tablespoon freshly squeezed
    lemon juice or white wine
    vinegar
1 shallot, minced (about
    1 tablespoon)
$\frac{1}{4}$ teaspoon kosher or fine sea salt

2 large egg yolks
$\frac{1}{2}$ cup (1 stick) butter or
    dairy-free butter substitute,
    melted
2 tablespoons fresh tarragon,
    minced

Place the lemon juice or white wine vinegar in a blender with the shallot and salt. Let sit for 2 to 3 minutes to allow the flavors to meld. Add the egg yolks and blend. With the blender running, remove the plastic insert from the blender top and add the melted butter slowly. Add the minced tarragon and blend to combine.

Chocolate-Strawberry Fool

½ cup semisweet chocolate chips	½ teaspoon pure vanilla extract
½ cup heavy whipping cream	¾ cup sliced strawberries

Place the chocolate chips in a microwave-safe bowl and microwave on high power for about 1 minute, or until most of the chips have melted, stirring every 30 seconds. Stir the chips well until smooth and glassy. Let cool. Alternatively you can place the chocolate chips in a heatproof bowl and place over a pan of simmering water until melted, making sure the bottom of the pan does not touch the simmering water.

While the chocolate cools, whip the cream and vanilla until stiff peaks form. Fold the cooled chocolate into the whipped cream with a spatula until combined; the mixture will have some streaks of darker chocolate; this is OK. Divide half of the mixture between two small dessert bowls or wineglasses. Reserve four strawberry slices for garnish and layer the rest over the chocolate. Top with the remaining chocolate cream. Garnish by sticking the strawberry halves into the cream, wide side down, and close together so they form a heart. Refrigerate until serving time.

In-Laws for Dinner

MENU

Pistachio-Cranberry-Goat Cheese-Stuffed Pork Tenderloin

Roasted Sweet Potato Wedges

Simple Green Salad

Almost Instant Nutella Mousse

When the in-laws, or anyone else you desperately need to impress, come to dinner, it is good to have a fancy schmancy recipe or two that look pretty, seem complicated and "gourmet" but, in truth, could not be simpler. The Pistachio-Cranberry-Goat Cheese–Stuffed Pork Tenderloin falls into that category. With little hands-on preparation time and about 20 minutes in the oven, this dish is special enough for even the most important of people and yet easy enough for a Wednesday night. With a main course this special, all you really need to add is some roasted sweet potatoes (or any roasted vegetable, really) and a perfect salad.

I have heard it said that even if people don't remember what they had for dinner, they will remember dessert. Mousse is a dessert everyone will remember fondly, especially when it is Nutella mousse. Normally a mousse takes hours to set up properly, but with my secret ingredient this mousse is set and ready to eat in about 15 minutes.

Quick-Cook Strategy

- If you are uncomfortable butterflying the pork tenderloin you can always have the butcher do it, but really it could not be easier. And, by the way, in case you don't normally have kitchen twine on hand, I have found that the butcher will always give you a length of it for the asking.
- Preheat the oven and remove the pork from the refrigerator and let sit at room temperature for 10 minutes to take the chill off. Also remove the goat cheese and set aside at room temperature to soften.
- Prepare the mousse and refrigerate it until serving time. Personally I think this mousse is perfect as is, but if you really need to impress, whip up some cream, add a dollop to each serving, and top with a berry or two.
- If you grind the pistachios used for rolling the tenderloin before making the filling, then there is no need to clean the food processor in between.
- The sweet potatoes and pork tenderloin will roast at the same temperature for roughly the same amount of time, but the meat needs to rest for 10 minutes before serving, so put the potatoes in the oven about 5 or 10 minutes after putting in the pork tenderloin.
- While the tenderloin and potatoes are roasting, prepare the lettuce for the salad and make the dressing. Toss the salad just before serving.

Pistachio-Cranberry-Goat Cheese–Stuffed Pork Tenderloin

¾ cups raw, unsalted pistachios
¼ cup dried cranberries
1 garlic clove
4 ounces goat cheese, at room temperature

One 1½- to 2-pound pork tenderloin
Kosher or fine sea salt
Freshly ground black pepper
2 to 3 tablespoons vegetable oil

Preheat the oven to 400 degrees. Toast ¼ cup of the pistachios in a small, dry skillet over medium-high heat until they are toasted and fragrant, about 3 minutes. Set aside to cool slightly. Grind the remaining ½ cup pistachios in a food processor until they resemble coarse cornmeal. Pour onto a plate and set aside.

Put the toasted pistachios into the food processor (no need to clean out the processor first) along with the dried cranberries and garlic. Pulse several times until the mixture is evenly ground. Add the goat cheese and pulse to combine well.

To butterfly the pork tenderloin, place it on a cutting board and slice it lengthwise almost all the way through, then open it out like a book. Season the inside of the meat with salt and pepper. Spread the pistachio-cranberry-goat cheese mixture evenly on the meat, leaving about a ½-inch border. Roll up the tenderloin lengthwise and tie with butcher's twine at 2-inch intervals. Roll the tied tenderloin in the ground pistachios, pressing the pistachios into the meat, until it is fully coated.

In an ovenproof skillet just large enough to hold the tenderloin, heat the oil until smoking hot. Place the tenderloin in the skillet and sear it on all sides for 1 to 2 minutes, or until browned. Place the skillet into the oven and roast the tenderloin for 15 to 20 minutes, or until the pork is cooked through. The temperature on an instant-read thermometer should register 145 degrees for medium (still pink on the inside) and 160 degrees for well-done.

Remove the tenderloin from the oven, transfer to a serving platter, cover loosely with aluminum foil, and let rest for 10 minutes. Slice and serve.

Roasted Sweet Potato Wedges

4 medium (about 2 pounds) sweet potatoes	½ teaspoon freshly ground black pepper
2 tablespoons olive oil	½ teaspoon paprika
1 teaspoon kosher or fine sea salt, plus more for sprinkling	

Preheat the oven to 400 degrees.

Scrub the sweet potatoes and cut each potato lengthwise into 8 wedges. Place on a rimmed baking sheet and toss with the olive oil, salt, pepper, and paprika to coat. Roast for 20 minutes, or until the potatoes are browned and tender. Flip the potato wedges twice with a spatula while roasting to ensure even browning. Sprinkle with a little more salt and serve.

Simple Green Salad

1 head butter lettuce	½ teaspoon kosher or fine sea
1 tablespoon freshly squeezed	salt
lemon juice	¼ teaspoon freshly ground black
3 tablespoons olive oil	pepper

Remove each leaf of the lettuce from the core and remove the large rib on the outer leaves. Tear larger leaves gently, leave the smaller ones whole. Rinse under plenty of cold running water. Dry the leaves very well using a salad spinner if you have one. Place in a salad bowl.

Whisk together the lemon juice, olive oil, salt, and pepper. Just before serving, pour the dressing over the lettuce and toss gently.

Almost Instant Nutella Mousse

One 7-ounce container
    marshmallow creme
    (Marshmallow Fluff)
¹/₂ cup Nutella

¹/₄ cup water
1 cup heavy whipping cream
1 teaspoon pure vanilla extract

Put the marshmallow creme, Nutella, and water in a medium saucepan. Place over low heat and cook, stirring until the marshmallow creme and Nutella are melted and fully combined. Remove from the heat, transfer to a metal bowl, and place in the freezer for 5 to 10 minutes to cool. While the mixture is cooling, whip the cream and vanilla until soft peaks form. Fold the cooled mixture into the cream until fully combined and divide equally among four serving bowls. Refrigerate for at least 15 minutes before serving.

Cinco de Mayo

• Dairy-Free

MENU

Mexico City Broil

Easy Mexican Rice

Quick Black Beans

Dairy-Free Coconut Pie

The fifth of May is Independence Day for the nation of Mexico. In my opinion any day that includes a Mexican feast is a day worth celebrating regardless of what your national heritage happens to be.

Mexico City Broil is really just a flank steak (also sold as London broil) with a Mexican twist. If you have time, whip up the marinade and let it languish in the refrigerator all day. If not, even a few minutes of marinating will tenderize the meat and add tremendous flavor.

Start this meal off with some corn tortilla chips and salsa and a pitcher of margaritas, and you have not only a feast but also a fiesta!

Serves 6

Quick-Cook Strategy

- Start by preheating the oven and getting the coconut flakes toasting for the coconut pie.
- While the coconut flakes are toasting, get all your vegetables and herbs chopped and all the limes juiced at one time; this will save time and make cleanup easier.
- Next get the flank steak marinating and put the rice in the microwave. These are things that take some time but no great hands-on effort.
- Get the coconut pie chilling and then you are ready to grill the flank steak and make the pico de gallo and the black beans.
- Heat some corn tortillas to serve along with the meal, if desired.

Mexico City Broil

1 jalapeño pepper, seeds and
   veins removed, finely minced

2 garlic cloves, finely minced

1 teaspoon ground cumin

Juice of 2 limes

1/2 cup olive oil

Kosher or fine sea salt

Freshly ground black pepper

One 1 1/2- to 2-pound flank steak

2 large tomatoes, seeded and
   chopped

1/2 small onion, finely chopped

1 avocado, chopped

1 small handful fresh cilantro,
   chopped

Mix together half the minced jalapeño pepper, garlic, cumin, juice of 1 lime, olive oil, and a large pinch of salt and pepper. Put the flank steak in a large food storage bag or glass baking dish and pour the marinade over, turning to coat the steak. Let marinate anywhere from a few minutes up to 12 hours, turning the meat over a couple of times. If marinating for more than 30 minutes, refrigerate. Let the steak sit at room temperature for about 10 minutes before cooking to take the chill off.

Preheat a grill, grill pan, or broiler.

Grill the meat, turning it once, for 6 to 7 minutes per side, or until an instant-read thermometer registers 125 to 135 degrees. Let the meat rest for 10 minutes, then cut across the grain into thin slices.

While the meat is resting, prepare the pico de gallo. Mix together the remaining jalapeño, tomatoes, onion, avocado, cilantro, and juice of 1 lime. Season the mixture with salt and pepper to taste. Serve as a garnish for the flank steak.

Easy Mexican Rice

2 tablespoons olive oil

½ cup finely chopped onions

1 cup arborio rice

One 15-ounce can chopped tomatoes (I like to use fire-roasted tomatoes)

½ teaspoon ground cumin

1 garlic clove

1 jalapeño pepper, finely chopped (optional)

Approximately 1 cup gluten-free chicken stock

Heat the olive oil in a large skillet over medium-high heat. Add the chopped onions and cook until soft but not brown, about 3 minutes. Add the rice and cook, stirring, for 2 more minutes; the rice will start to look translucent. Put the onion-rice mixture into a microwave-safe casserole dish with a lid.

Put the chopped tomatoes with their juice, ground cumin, garlic, and jalapeño, if using, into a blender and blend until smooth. Add enough gluten-free chicken stock to make 3 cups of liquid and blend.

Add the tomato-chicken stock mixture to the rice, stir, and microwave on high 18 to 20 minutes. Stir 3 times while cooking. Remove from microwave, stir, replace the lid, and let stand 5 minutes.

Quick Black Beans

1 tablespoon olive oil

1 medium onion, chopped

2 garlic cloves, minced

Two 15-ounce cans black beans, rinsed and drained

2 cups gluten-free chicken stock or water

2 tablespoons chopped fresh cilantro

Juice of 1 lime

Kosher or fine sea salt

Freshly ground black pepper

1/4 teaspoon cayenne pepper (optional)

Heat the olive oil in a large saucepan over medium heat. Add the onion and sauté until soft, about 5 minutes. Add the garlic and sauté 1 minute. Add the black beans and chicken stock or water, increase the heat, and bring to a boil. Reduce the heat and simmer, uncovered, until most of the liquid has evaporated, about 5 minutes. Add the cilantro and lime juice and season to taste with salt and black pepper. Add the cayenne pepper if you prefer more heat.

Dairy-Free Coconut Pie

1³⁄₄ cups sweetened, flaked coconut

1 cup gluten-free, graham-style crumbs

5 tablespoons coconut oil, melted (or nondairy butter substitute such as Earth Balance)

One 13.5-ounce can unsweetened coconut milk, shaken well

¹⁄₄ cup firmly packed brown sugar

¹⁄₄ cup tapioca starch or cornstarch

¹⁄₄ teaspoon kosher or fine sea salt

1 teaspoon pure vanilla extract

Preheat the oven to 350 degrees. Spray a 9-inch pie plate lightly with gluten-free, nonstick cooking spray.

Place 1 ¼ cups of the coconut on a rimmed baking sheet and spread it into an even layer. Set the remaining ½ cup aside. Toast the coconut in the oven until it is fragrant and lightly browned, 8 to 10 minutes, stirring once or twice during the toasting for even browning. Reserve ¼ cup of the toasted coconut for the garnish.

In a mixing bowl, combine the remaining 1 cup of the toasted coconut with the graham-style crumbs and the coconut oil. Press into a 9-inch pie plate, making sure to press the mixture up the sides as well as on the bottom. Place in the freezer to cool and harden while preparing the filling.

In a medium saucepan, whisk together the coconut milk, brown sugar, tapioca starch or cornstarch, and salt. Heat the mixture over medium heat, stirring constantly, until it thickens, about 3 minutes. Stir in the vanilla. You can press the mixture through a fine-mesh strainer if you like to make sure there are no lumps. Stir in the reserved ½ cup of the untoasted coconut flakes. Pour the mixture into the prepared pie plate. Let the tart cool in the refrigerator until ready to serve. Garnish with the reserved toasted coconut flakes.

Lazy Summer Afternoon Party

~~~~~~~~~~~~~~~~~~

MENU

Oven-Fried Chicken

Chipotle Potato Salad

Roasted Corn with Chili-Lime Butter

Creamy Coleslaw

Cookies and Cream No-Bake Cheesecakes

~~~~~~~~~~~~~~~~~~

This is a great menu for the Fourth of July, Labor Day, or any summer day when you want to have family and friends over for a casual, no-stress party.

Toss in some lemonade, iced tea, and maybe some gluten-free beer and you have an old-fashioned Sunday dinner with a few new twists.

Serves 6

Quick-Cook Strategy

- Have the butcher cut the chicken for you or buy one already cut into 8 or 9 pieces.
- Preheat the oven to 375 degrees.
- Take the butter for the corn out of the refrigerator and let it soften at room temperature.
- If you don't have time to let the cream cheese soften at room temperature, microwave it at 30 percent power in 10-second intervals, but be careful to check it after each interval, microwaves heat from the inside out. It should take about 30 seconds to soften.
- Make the cheesecakes first and refrigerate them. Using a handheld mixer will save some time, and if you whip the cream first you don't have to clean the beaters before beating the cheese and sugar.
- Bring the potatoes to a boil on the stovetop. As always, a covered pot will boil faster. Keep the pot covered while cooking the potatoes.
- I blend an entire can of chipotle peppers in adobe sauce in the blender until pureed and then store them in a clean, sterilized jar in the refrigerator for when I want to add chipotle to a recipe. This way I can always spoon a little into a recipe when I need to without having to chop or blend the individual chipotles. Also, since I rarely use a whole can at one time, this extends the shelf life.
- Put the chicken and corn in the oven at the same time. Place the chicken on the top shelf of the oven and the corn directly on the oven racks. Make the coleslaw and chili-lime butter while the chicken and corn are baking.

Oven-Fried Chicken

2 cups dried onion flakes (dehydrated onions)	1 teaspoon paprika
6 ounces shredded or grated Parmesan cheese	1 teaspoon garlic powder
2 teaspoons kosher or fine sea salt	2 large eggs
1 teaspoon freshly ground black pepper	2 to 3 dashes of hot sauce
	One 3- to 4-pound whole broiler-fryer chicken, cut into 8 or 9 pieces

Preheat the oven to 375 degrees. Spray a baking sheet with gluten-free, nonstick cooking spray.

Place the onion flakes, cheese, salt, pepper, paprika, and garlic powder in a food processor fitted with the steel blade and process for 1 minute. Pour the mixture into a large freezer storage bag.

Beat the eggs lightly with the hot sauce. Dip the chicken pieces in the egg and then drop them into the bag with the coating mix, a few pieces at a time. Place on the prepared baking sheet and spray lightly with more cooking spray. Bake for 30 minutes, or until golden brown and the juices run clear when the chicken is pierced with a sharp knife. Serve the chicken hot, cold, or at room temperature.

Chipotle Potato Salad

2½ pounds baby red potatoes, cut into 1½-inch pieces
1 chipotle pepper in adobe sauce with 1½ teaspoons sauce (or 1 tablespoon pureed chipotle)
3 tablespoons honey
3 tablespoons apple cider vinegar
½ teaspoon salt
¼ teaspoon freshly ground black pepper
⅓ cup olive oil
½ cup fresh cilantro leaves, roughly chopped or torn

Place the potatoes in a large pot of generously salted cold water, cover, and bring to a boil. Cook until the potatoes are fork-tender, 10 to 12 minutes.

While the potatoes are boiling, make the dressing. Place the chipotle pepper and sauce in a blender with the honey, vinegar, salt, and black pepper. Blend until smooth. Remove the plastic insert from the blender top and, with the machine running, slowly pour in the olive oil.

Drain the potatoes and return them to the hot pot. Add the dressing and stir to combine. Set aside to cool. Just before serving, add the cilantro and stir to combine. This salad is best served warm.

Roasted Corn with Chili-Lime Butter

6 ears of corn in the husks	Finely grated zest of 1 lime
6 tablespoons (3/4 stick) unsalted butter, softened	2 teaspoons chili powder

Preheat the oven to 375 degrees. Place the corn directly on the oven rack and roast for 30 minutes.

While the corn is roasting, prepare the butter. Mix the butter with the lime zest and chili powder. When the corn is done, peel back the husks, remove the strings, and serve hot with the butter.

Creamy Coleslaw

½ cup good-quality mayonnaise

¼ cup sour cream

¼ cup apple cider vinegar

2 tablespoons honey, agave
    nectar, or sugar

1 teaspoon kosher or fine sea salt

½ teaspoon freshly ground black
    pepper

16 ounces preshredded coleslaw
    mix with cabbage and carrots

In a large mixing bowl, whisk together the mayonnaise, sour cream, vinegar, honey, salt, and pepper until smooth.

Add the coleslaw mix and stir to combine. Refrigerate until serving time.

Cookies and Cream
No-Bake Cheesecakes

21 gluten-free, chocolate sandwich creme cookies (such as
KinniToos)

4 tablespoons melted butter

1 cup heavy whipping cream

8 ounces cream cheese, softened

1/2 cup sugar

1 teaspoon pure vanilla extract

Place paper liners in the cups of a 12-cup standard muffin pan.

Take 3 of the cookies, cut them in quarters, and set aside for garnish. Place 12 cookies in a plastic freezer bag and pound them with a rolling pin until they turn into fine crumbs. Combine the crumbs with the melted butter and divide the mixture equally among the muffin cups and press down firmly and evenly. Place the remaining cookies in the bag and break them up so that there are bigger pieces of cookie as well as some crumbs.

Using a handheld mixer, whip the cream on high speed until stiff peaks form. Place the cream cheese, sugar, and vanilla in a large mixing bowl and beat on high speed until smooth and well blended. Fold in the whipped cream and the crushed cookie pieces. Spoon the mixture into the muffin cups. Place one of the quartered cookies on top of each cheesecake. Refrigerate until serving time.

Quick Thanksgiving

MENU

Roasted Cornish Game Hens

Skillet Dressing

Cranberry Gravy

Maple Mashed Sweet Potatoes

Oven-Roasted Balsamic Onion Green Beans

Pumpkin Mousse Pie

Sometimes it just doesn't make sense to prepare a huge Thanksgiving feast. When there is only a handful of guests at the table, a huge turkey seems extravagant and wasteful. In this instance, a smaller, more manageable dinner is more appropriate. This is also a great meal for other times of the year when you crave all the flavors of Thanksgiving without all the fuss.

I got the idea of serving Roasted Cornish Game Hens for Thanksgiving from my father. One year it was just the two of us but he still wanted the day to seem special. The best thing about the game hens is that each diner gets their own drumstick!

Quick-Cook Strategy

- Preheat the oven to 350 degrees for the pie crust. Prepare the crust and while it is in the oven, make the filling. Once the crust has baked, crank the oven up to 450 degrees.
- Get all your vegetables prepped, chopped, minced, and sliced for the entire menu; this will make the flow of cooking go so much better.
- Cut up the game hens and season and brown them so they are ready to go in the oven.
- Get the sweet potatoes cooking on the stovetop. If they are done before you are ready to mash them, they can wait for you off the heat in the hot water.
- The green beans and game hens can go into the oven at the same time.
- Use the same skillet you browned the game hens in to make the Cranberry Gravy. Just drain the oil and wipe it clean with a paper towel. This saves time with cleanup later.
- The Skillet Dressing and Cranberry Gravy can be made while the hens and beans are in the oven. Start the dressing first as it takes a bit longer.

Roasted Cornish Game Hens

3 Cornish game hens	2 teaspoons poultry seasoning
1½ teaspoons kosher or fine sea salt	2 tablespoons olive oil
1 teaspoon freshly ground black pepper	

Preheat the oven to 450 degrees.

Remove everything from the cavities of the game hens and either discard or reserve for another use. Halve the hens by cutting each of them along both sides of the backbone with scissors or kitchen shears. Cut along one side of the breastbone to separate it into two halves. Rinse the halves and pat dry with paper towels. Combine the salt, pepper, and poultry seasoning and rub all over the game hen halves.

Heat the oil in a large skillet over medium-high heat and add the hen halves skin side down. Sauté in batches (do not crowd the pan) until golden brown, about 4 minutes. Turn and sauté the opposite side for 2 minutes. Transfer the hens to a roasting pan, skin side up, and roast, uncovered, for 20 minutes, or until an instant-read thermometer inserted at the thickest part of the breast registers 165 degrees, and the juices run clear when the hens are pierced with a sharp knife. Cover with aluminum foil and let rest for 5 to 10 minutes before serving.

Skillet Dressing

4 tablespoons (½ stick) unsalted
   butter
1 medium onion, finely chopped
2 celery stalks, finely chopped
2 garlic cloves, minced
1½ teaspoons poultry
   seasoning

½ teaspoon freshly ground black
   pepper
1¼ to 1½ cups gluten-free
   chicken stock
2 cups gluten-free, panko-style
   bread crumbs
Kosher or fine sea salt, if needed

Melt the butter in large skillet over medium heat. Add the onion and celery and cook until they soften, about 5 minutes. Add the garlic, poultry seasoning, and pepper and cook for 1 minute. Add 1¼ cups of the chicken stock and simmer for 5 minutes. Add the bread crumbs and stir to combine. Remove from the heat, cover the pan, and let rest for 8 to 10 minutes. If the dressing seems too dry, add a little more chicken stock. Taste and add more salt, if needed.

Cranberry Gravy

12 ounces (about 3 cups) fresh or frozen whole cranberries

1 cup freshly squeezed orange juice

1½ cups gluten-free chicken stock

⅓ cup sugar

Kosher or fine sea salt

Freshly ground black pepper

Combine the cranberries, orange juice, chicken stock, and sugar in a large skillet and bring to a boil over high heat. Continue to cook, uncovered, stirring occasionally, until the liquid is reduced by half and the berries pop, 8 to 10 minutes. Season to taste with a little salt and pepper.

Maple Mashed Sweet Potatoes

3 pounds sweet potatoes, peeled and chopped	3 tablespoons unsalted butter
1 teaspoon kosher or fine sea salt	3 tablespoons maple syrup
½ teaspoon freshly ground black pepper	4 to 6 tablespoons cream, half-and-half, or milk

Put the cut-up sweet potatoes in a large pan and cover with cold water. Cover the pan and place over high heat, bring to a boil, and cook until tender, about 10 minutes. Drain the sweet potatoes and return them to the hot pot. Return the pot to the stovetop over medium heat and cook, stirring constantly, for about 1 minute to evaporate excess moisture. Season with salt and pepper and mash the sweet potatoes coarsely. Add the butter and maple syrup and mash to combine. Add the cream, half-and-half, or milk, a little at a time, and mash until you reach the desired consistency.

Oven-Roasted Balsamic Onion Green Beans

1½ pounds green beans, stem
    ends snapped off
1 medium red onion, peeled,
    halved, and each half cut into
    6 wedges
2 tablespoons olive oil

1 teaspoon kosher or fine sea salt
½ teaspoon freshly ground black
    pepper
2 tablespoons balsamic vinegar
2 teaspoons honey

Preheat the oven to 450 degrees. Line a rimmed baking sheet with aluminum foil.

Place the green beans and onion wedges on the prepared baking sheet and toss with the olive oil, salt, and pepper. Spread the vegetables out into an even layer and roast for 10 minutes.

In a small bowl, combine the balsamic vinegar with the honey. When the beans and onion have roasted for 10 minutes, remove them from the oven, pour the vinegar-honey mixture over the top, and toss with tongs to coat. Return the baking sheet to the oven and continue to roast for 12 to 15 minutes, or until the onion and beans are dark golden brown in spots and the beans start to shrivel. Transfer to a serving dish and serve immediately.

Pumpkin Mousse Pie

One 8-ounce package gluten-free graham crackers (or 1½ cups gluten-free, graham-style crumbs, firmly packed)

¼ cup granulated sugar

6 tablespoons (¾ stick) unsalted butter, melted

¼ teaspoon kosher or fine sea salt

4 ounces cream cheese, at room temperature

One 15-ounce can pumpkin puree

½ cup firmly packed brown sugar

2 teaspoons whiskey (optional)

1 to 2 teaspoons pure vanilla extract

½ teaspoon ground cinnamon

Pinch of ground cloves

A grating of nutmeg

2½ cups heavy whipping cream

2 to 3 tablespoons Heath English Toffee Bits

Preheat the oven to 350 degrees.

Break the graham crackers up and place in food processor fitted with the steel blade and grind into crumbs. Or place the crackers in a plastic food bag and crush with a rolling pin. Combine the crushed crumbs with the granulated sugar, melted butter, and salt and mix well. Press the mixture into a 9-inch pie plate, pressing it down firmly and making sure to press the mixture up the sides as well as on the bottom. Bake for 8 minutes. Remove from oven, let cool 5 minutes, then put it in the freezer for 10 minutes to finish cooling and firm up.

Using a handheld mixer, beat the cream cheese, pumpkin, brown sugar, whiskey (if using), vanilla (if not using whiskey use 2 teaspoons, otherwise use 1 teaspoon), cinnamon, cloves, and nutmeg until smooth and creamy.

In a clean bowl, using clean beaters, whip the cream until soft peaks form. Mix a little of the cream into the pumpkin mixture, then fold in the rest. Fill the cooled pie with the mixture and smooth the top. Refrigerate until serving time. Just before serving, garnish the top of the pie with the toffee bits.

Roast Beef Dinner

MENU

Roasted Beef Tenderloin with Red Onion Gravy

Mini Yorkshire Puddings

Roasted Brussels Sprouts

Glazed Carrots

Quick Black Forest Trifle

Christmas dinner for me means roast beef. Fortunately, roasting a tenderloin could not be easier, is practically foolproof, and is much quicker than using other cuts of beef for roasting. Yorkshire pudding is a traditional British accompaniment to roast beef. It is typically made with the meat drippings of a standing rib roast. Olive oil is used in place of beef fat in this recipe, and the puddings are quickly cooked in a muffin pan.

The rest of the meal follows in the same British tradition. Best of all, this entire meal can be made in an hour. After all, who wants to spend Christmas Day slaving in the kitchen?

Quick-Cook Strategy

- Preheat the oven and remove the tenderloin from the refrigerator to take the chill off. Everything that is cooked in the oven is cooked at the same temperature.
- Prepare the trifle and refrigerate until time for dessert.
- Prepare the Brussels sprouts and the roast beef and place them in the oven at the same time; they take roughly the same amount of time to roast. Transfer the Brussels sprouts to an ovenproof serving bowl and cover with aluminum foil to keep warm; if needed they can be reheated in the oven briefly just before serving.
- While the beef and Brussels sprouts are roasting, prepare the batter for the Yorkshire puddings. Put the pan for the puddings into the oven to preheat as soon as you remove the beef and Brussels sprouts; this way they will be done at the same time as the roast beef is served. You can also prepare the gravy at this time, keep it in the pan, and warm it back up on the stovetop, if needed, just before serving.
- The carrots are cooked on the stovetop and can be made while the puddings are baking.

Roasted Beef Tenderloin with Red Onion Gravy

One 2½- to 3-pound center cut beef tenderloin, trimmed
1 tablespoon olive oil
2 teaspoons kosher or fine sea salt
1 teaspoon freshly ground black pepper

4 tablespoons (½ stick) unsalted butter
1 medium red onion, halved and thinly sliced (about 1 cup)
¾ cup dry red wine
2 sprigs fresh rosemary
¾ cup gluten-free beef stock

Preheat the oven to 450 degrees. Line a 13×9-inch roasting pan with foil.

Brush the tenderloin with the olive oil. Combine the salt and pepper on a plate or on a cutting board and roll the tenderloin in it to season it on all sides. Place the tenderloin in the prepared roasting pan and roast approximately 25 minutes for rare (120 to 125 degrees on an instant-read thermometer) or approximately 30 minutes for medium rare (125 to 130 degrees on an instant-read thermometer). Remove the roast from the oven and wrap it with the foil you covered the roasting pan with. Let the meat rest on a cutting board for 15 minutes.

While the meat is resting, prepare the gravy. Melt 2 tablespoons of the butter in a large skillet over medium heat. Add the onion and cook, stirring often, until it is soft and starts to brown, about 10 minutes. Add the wine and rosemary and increase the heat to medium-high. Boil until the liquid has reduced to ½ cup, about 3 minutes. Add the beef stock and continue to boil until reduced to 1 cup, about 5 minutes. Reduce the heat to low, remove and discard the rosemary sprigs, and stir in the remaining 2 tablespoons of butter until the butter has melted and the gravy is glossy.

Remove the foil from the meat, pour any accumulated meat juices into the gravy, and stir in. Taste the gravy and add more salt and pepper, if needed. Slice the beef thinly and place on a serving platter. Ladle a little of the gravy over top and serve the rest on the side in a gravy boat.

Mini Yorkshire Puddings

2 tablespoons olive oil	½ teaspoon kosher or fine sea salt
2 large eggs	1 cup Sweet Rice Flour Blend
1 cup whole milk	(page 17)

Preheat the oven to 450 degrees. Put ½ teaspoon olive oil in each cup of a standard 12-cup muffin pan. Place the muffin pan in the oven for 5 minutes to preheat the pan and the oil.

In a medium mixing bowl, whisk the eggs well. Add the milk and salt and whisk to combine. Add the flour, a little at a time, whisking well after each addition. Pour the mixture into a pitcher or large measuring cup with a spout.

Carefully remove the muffin pan from the oven and pour some batter into each cup, filling each halfway. Bake the Yorkshire puddings for 14 minutes, or until puffed and golden brown. While they are baking, refrain from opening the oven door. Remove the puddings from the pan and serve immediately.

Roasted Brussels Sprouts

1½ pounds Brussels sprouts	½ teaspoon freshly ground black
2 tablespoons olive oil	pepper
¾ teaspoon kosher or fine sea salt	

Preheat the oven to 450 degrees.

Trim the bottom ends off the Brussels sprouts and cut in half lengthwise. Place on a rimmed baking sheet, add the olive oil, salt, and pepper, and toss to coat. Spread the Brussels sprouts out in an even layer and roast for 15 to 20 minutes, or until they are fork-tender. Transfer to a serving bowl, sprinkle with a little more kosher salt, if desired, and serve.

Glazed Carrots

Two 1-pound packages peeled
  baby carrots
2 tablespoons unsalted butter
¼ cup firmly packed light brown
  sugar

½ teaspoon kosher or fine sea
  salt
¼ teaspoon freshly ground black
  pepper

Put the carrots in a medium saucepan with water to cover. Cover the pan and bring to a boil. Reduce the heat and simmer 10 to 15 minutes until the carrots are tender. Drain the water from the pan, return the carrots to the saucepan, and place back on the heat. Add the butter, brown sugar, salt, and pepper, stir to coat the carrots, and cook until glazed. Transfer to a serving bowl.

Quick Black Forest Trifle

One 1-ounce package instant vanilla pudding mix (JELL-O brand or other brand that is gluten-free)

1½ cups cold milk

6 gluten-free chocolate glazed donuts, thawed

Two 15-ounce cans pitted dark sweet cherries in heavy syrup

One 8-ounce container whipped topping, thawed

Cocoa powder for dusting

Whisk together the pudding mix and cold milk until the mixture is smooth and starts to thicken. Set aside.

Cut the donuts in half horizontally and then cut each half into quarters. Layer half the cut donuts into a medium-sized glass serving bowl or divide among 6 large wine goblets or dessert bowls.

Drain the syrup from the cans of cherries, reserving the juice of one can. Spoon 3 tablespoons of reserved juice on the cut donuts, then top with one can of cherries. Spoon half of the pudding on top of the cherries and top with half of the whipped topping. Repeat layers. Cover with plastic wrap and refrigerate until ready to serve. Can be made up to a day ahead. Dust with cocoa powder before serving.

Get Up and Go

NO ONE WHO knows me would ever accuse me of being a morning person. I really don't like to do anything, including speak, until the caffeine from my inordinately large cup of coffee kicks in. However, I know how important it is to feed our families properly in the morning and fuel them for the day's adventures.

While it is easy to pour some milk over a bowl of gluten-free cereal, or scramble a couple eggs in the morning, variety is essential if you want your family to eat breakfast.

This chapter offers some breakfast ideas that will get your day off to a good start, stress-free. After all, there is no need for stress first thing in the morning.

Piña Colada Smoothie

For some people, the thought of eating solid food first thing in the morning is just more than they can bear. But starting the day without food is like trying to drive a car without gas. Smoothies are the answer. This is a delicious morning "cocktail" with a secret stash of extra fiber thanks to the flaxseed meal. No one will know it's there (especially if you use golden flaxseed meal) but it will not only boost the fiber content but also help thicken the smoothie as well.

Depending on the sweetness of your pineapple, you may want to sweeten the smoothie up a bit by adding a teaspoon or so of honey, agave nectar, or even better, two Medjool dates, pitted and chopped. Buying a peeled and cored pineapple will speed your morning along.

- Dairy-Free
- Sugar-Free

Serves 1 to 2

---

1 cup coconut milk

1 cup fresh pineapple chunks

1 ripe banana

3 tablespoons flaxseed meal

1 tiny pinch of kosher or fine sea salt

5 to 6 ice cubes

Place all the ingredients into the jar of a blender and whirl until fully blended and smooth. Drink immediately.

Breakfast Quesadilla

• Dairy-Free
Adaptable

• Sugar-Free

Serves 1

There is just something fun about eating quesadillas for breakfast; it breaks up the routine and, in my experience, anything kids can dip or eat with their hands is good by them.

The trick to making this work is to make a thin omelet out of the eggs first and then sandwich it between the tortillas with some cheese or dairy-free cheese holding it all together. You can add to this basic recipe as you see fit—a smear of black beans would be great as would diced green chili peppers, sliced scallions, chopped tomatoes, or sliced black olives. And for me, salsa is a must.

2 large eggs	⅓ cup grated cheese or dairy-
Kosher or fine sea salt and	free cheese
pepper	2 to 3 tablespoons salsa
2 corn tortillas	

Heat a 6-inch, nonstick skillet over medium heat. Whisk the eggs together with a pinch of salt and pepper until fully combined. Spray the hot pan with some gluten-free, nonstick cooking spray. Pour in the eggs, tilting the pan to spread the mixture evenly. Cook for about 1 minute, or until the eggs are cooked around the edges and almost set. Slide a spatula around the edges to loosen and flip the omelet over and cook for another 30 seconds, or until the eggs are cooked through. Transfer the omelet from the pan to a plate.

Spray the skillet with a little more nonstick cooking spray and press one tortilla down into the skillet. Top with half the cheese, place the omelet on top of the cheese, sprinkle the remaining cheese on top of the egg, and top with the other tortilla. Spray the top of the tortilla lightly with nonstick cooking spray. Cook the quesadilla for 1 minute, or until the bottom tortilla starts to brown and the cheese starts to melt. Flip the quesadilla over and cook for another minute or so, pressing down with a spatula to help the cheese melt. Cut the quesadilla into wedges and serve with salsa.

Whole Grain Overnight Porridge

~~~~~~

• Dairy-Free

• Sugar-Free

Serves 8 to 10

This is a healthy, hearty, stick-to-your-ribs dish to start the day that seems almost decadent to eat; it has the taste and texture of a creamy pudding. And the best part is that there is nothing to do in the morning but scoop it out. You place all the ingredients in a slow cooker right before bed and it is there waiting for you when you wake.

This recipe makes a big batch, but it reheats well in the microwave. Or you can halve the amounts of the ingredients if you have a small slow cooker.

Serve with some more almond milk, chopped dried fruit, and possibly a sprinkling of slivered almonds, if you like. I find this plenty sweet as is, but if you are like my husband, who has a quite pronounced sweet tooth, you can add some maple syrup, raw turbinado sugar, or brown sugar to taste. For a tropical version, substitute coconut milk for the almond milk, and add dried tropical fruits in place of the apricots.

1 cup whole millet
½ cup prerinsed quinoa (if you can't find prerinsed then place the quinoa in a very fine-mesh strainer and run cold water over it until the water runs clear)
½ cup gluten-free, steel-cut oats

1 teaspoon kosher or fine sea salt
1 cup dried apricots, coarsely chopped
10 Medjool dates, pitted and finely chopped
4 cups unsweetened almond milk
2 teaspoons pure vanilla extract

Spray the inside of a slow cooker with gluten-free, nonstick cooking spray. Add all the ingredients and stir. Cook on low for 8 hours. Stir well and serve.

Banana-Date Muffins

• Dairy-Free
Adaptable

• Sugar-Free

Makes 12
muffins

Muffins may not seem like a quick breakfast since they have to be baked, but these are so simple and your blender or food processor does most of the work for you. Since they only take a couple minutes to prepare, you can pop them in the oven, have a cup of coffee and a shower, and voila, breakfast is ready.

Dates and bananas make these muffins wonderfully sweet without having to add any refined sugar. You need not tell this to your kids; they will think they are getting away with eating dessert for breakfast.

These muffins do tend to stick to the paper liners a bit so if this bothers you get reusable silicone muffin baking liners.

³/₄ cup milk or dairy-free milk of
your choice
2 large eggs
2 bananas, peeled and cut into
chunks
8 Medjool dates, pitted and

coarsely chopped
4 tablespoons (¹/₂ stick) butter or
dairy-free butter substitute,
melted
2 cups Whole Grain Pancake and
Biscuit Mix (page 24)

Preheat the oven to 350 degrees. Line a standard 12-cup muffin pan with paper or silicone liners.

Place all ingredients for the muffins into a blender or food processor and process to combine. Divide the mixture among the prepared muffin cups (an ice cream scoop works well for this) and bake for 25 to 30 minutes, or until the muffins are golden brown and a toothpick inserted into the center comes out fairly clean. Let cool and serve.

Egg Florentine Cups

Ham, spinach, and egg all contained in a cute little package not unlike a muffin, these breakfast cups are elegant and easy. To make them really special, spoon on some *Easy Blender Béarnaise Sauce*. This recipe can easily be doubled if you are feeding a crowd; no need to increase the cooking time.

Look for extra-thin sliced ham in the deli section, and make sure the brand you buy is gluten-free.

- Dairy-Free Adaptable

- Sugar-Free

Makes 6 egg cups

6 slices extra-thin sliced ham	Freshly ground black pepper
1 teaspoon olive oil	2 or 3 gratings of nutmeg
1 garlic clove, peeled and lightly smashed	6 tablespoons grated Parmesan cheese (omit for dairy-free)
One 6-ounce package prewashed baby spinach	6 large eggs
Kosher or fine sea salt	Easy Blender Béarnaise Sauce (optional; page 123)

Preheat the oven to 375 degrees. Spray a standard 6-cup muffin pan liberally with gluten-free, nonstick cooking spray. Lay a slice of ham into each muffin cup and press to form a cup.

Heat the olive oil in a large skillet over medium-high heat. Add the garlic clove and cook until lightly browned, about 1 minute. Remove and discard the garlic. Increase the heat to high, add the spinach, a large pinch of salt and pepper, and the nutmeg. Cook, tossing constantly, until the spinach is wilted and any liquid has evaporated, 2 to 3 minutes. Divide the spinach among the ham-lined cups. If using the cheese, spoon in 1 tablespoon per cup. Break an egg into each cup, being careful not to break the yolks. Sprinkle each egg with a tiny pinch of salt and pepper. Bake for 15 minutes, or until the whites are firm but the yolks are still a little runny (if you do not like runny yolks, cook longer). Let cool for a minute and then run a dinner knife or small offset spatula around the edges and carefully remove from the pan. Serve immediately.

Vegan Breakfast Bars

- Dairy-Free

- Refined Sugar-Free

- Vegetarian/ Vegan

I am often hesitant to put the word "vegan" into the title of a recipe because I am afraid people who are not vegan will not try it out of prejudice. But since the same could be said for the words "gluten-free" I have come to terms with it. If you have the same concerns, just don't tell; these are so addictive no one will even think to ask.

Admittedly these bars cannot just be whipped up in minutes the morning you want to eat them because they bake for an hour, but actual preparation time is very short and they keep for a week if stored in an airtight container. Make them on a lazy weekend day and they will be there to grab and go on hectic workday mornings.

Use whatever dried fruit you like; in my family we are fond of apricots, cherries, and cranberries.

2½ cups certified gluten-free oats

1 cup sliced almonds

1 cup roasted seeds such as sunflower or pumpkin

1½ cups dried fruit, coarsely chopped

1 cup shredded coconut

½ teaspoon kosher or sea salt

One 13.5-ounce can unsweetened coconut milk, shaken well

½ cup agave nectar or maple syrup

3 tablespoons cornstarch, tapioca starch, or arrowroot powder

1 teaspoon pure vanilla extract

Preheat the oven to 250 degrees. Heavily spray a 12 × 9-inch baking dish with nonstick cooking spray.

In a large mixing bowl, combine the oats, almonds, seeds, dried fruit, coconut, and salt. In a small bowl, whisk together the coconut milk, agave or maple syrup, cornstarch (or tapioca starch or arrowroot powder), and vanilla. Add

Makes 12 bars

this to the oat mixture and mix well with a large spatula until fully combined. Spread the mixture into the prepared dish and press down firmly and evenly with the spatula (or your hands). Bake for 1 hour.

Let cool for 15 minutes, then run a sharp knife around the edges of the dish, and cut into twelve 3-inch squares. Let cool completely before removing from the pan.

Store in an airtight container or plastic food storage bag.

Pantry Raid

UNEXPECTED GUESTS? A meeting that ran late? Feeling under the weather but still have to feed hungry children? These are all things that can wreak havoc in our eating lives. A well-stocked pantry, as I have mentioned before, can be a lifesaver. No matter how organized we may be there are always times when we need to whip up something delicious to eat without the luxury of running to the store.

Included in this chapter are a few of my favorite "pantry raid" recipes; dishes that can be prepared by rummaging around a well-stocked pantry and freezer. These are also helpful when faced with a late-night attack of hunger; there is something so rewarding to be able to "shop" in your jammies right in your own kitchen.

Pistachio-Spinach Pesto

• Dairy-Free
Adaptable

• Vegetarian

Makes about
1 1/2 cups pesto

Pesto is one of those quick, versatile recipes you should master—not that it takes much effort to master. Throw some ingredients into a food processor, hit the "on" button, and you're there. Tossed with gluten-free pasta, you can have dinner on the table as quickly as it takes for the pasta to cook. Drizzled over sliced tomatoes and mozzarella cheese, you have a delicious Italian salad. Or put it in a serving bowl surrounded with fresh veggies, and you have a beautiful, healthy appetizer.

This version of pesto is more economical than the traditional recipe made with pine nuts since pistachios are less expensive, and the addition of spinach not only makes it healthier but also makes your pesto a beautiful green color. The lemon juice brightens the flavor and allows you to use less olive oil, thus making the recipe lower in fat.

1 cup shelled pistachios
2 cups spinach leaves
1/2 cup basil leaves
1/2 cup Parmesan cheese, grated
   (omit for dairy-free)
Finely grated zest and juice of 1
   lemon

1/4 teaspoon freshly ground black
   pepper
1/4 to 1/3 cup olive oil
Kosher salt

Put the pistachios in the bowl of a food processor fitted with the steel blade. Process until the nuts are coarsely ground. Add the spinach, basil, Parmesan cheese (if using), lemon zest and juice, black pepper, and 1/4 cup olive oil. Process until smooth. If the pesto is too thick, add a little more olive oil. Season to taste with a pinch of salt, if desired.

Black Bean Blender Soup

- Dairy-Free
Adaptable

- Vegetarian
Adaptable

Serves 4

There are few things more comforting and warming than a hearty black bean soup. What makes this dish even more comforting is that it takes mere minutes to make and the blender does most of the work. If you just don't have any limes on hand, the lime juice is not a must, but it needs to be said that it really brightens the flavor and adds freshness to the canned pantry items. Additionally, if you do not have the ingredients for the garnish on hand, it is not essential. A handful of corn tortilla chips on the side will complement the Southwestern flavors in this easy soup.

Two 15-ounce cans black beans, rinsed and drained
2 cups gluten-free chicken or vegetable stock
½ cup prepared salsa
1 teaspoon ground cumin
Kosher or fine sea salt
Freshly ground black pepper
Juice of 1 lime (optional)

GARNISH
Juice of ½ a lime (more or less)
½ cup sour cream (or dairy-free sour cream)
Sliced scallions, white and green parts, or cilantro leaves

Put one can of rinsed and drained black beans into a blender along with the chicken or vegetable stock, salsa, and ground cumin. Blend until smooth. Pour into a saucepan, add the remaining can of beans, and bring to a boil over medium heat. Season to taste with salt and pepper. Add the lime juice, if using, and stir to combine.

Stir some lime juice into the sour cream and in until smooth. Swirl some of the sour cream over the top of each serving and garnish with sliced scallions or cilantro.

Mexican Pumpkin Soup

This is a rich and creamy soup packed with flavor. The toasted pumpkin seeds add a touch of crunch. Store nuts and seeds in the freezer; this way they are always fresh and on hand.

- Dairy-Free

- Vegetarian Adaptable

Serves 6

½ cup pumpkin seeds

2 tablespoons olive oil

1 small onion, chopped

2 garlic cloves, minced

One 4-ounce can diced mild green chilies

2 teaspoons brown sugar

1 teaspoon ground cumin

½ teaspoon salt

¼ teaspoon freshly ground black pepper

¼ teaspoon red crushed pepper flakes (optional)

One 15-ounce can pureed pumpkin (not pumpkin pie mix)

2 cups gluten-free chicken or vegetable stock

One 13.5-ounce can unsweetened coconut milk, shaken well

In a dry skillet over medium-high heat, toast pumpkin seeds for about 3 minutes until browned and you can smell the oils being released. Set aside.

In a large saucepan, heat the olive oil over medium heat. Add the onion and sauté until translucent, about 5 minutes. Add the minced garlic and chopped chilies and sauté for 2 minutes. Add the brown sugar, cumin, salt, black pepper, and red pepper flakes if using and sauté for another minute, then add the pumpkin, chicken or vegetable stock, and coconut milk and stir well. Reduce the heat and cook until heated through, 5 to 6 minutes.

Process the soup in a blender in batches until smooth; do not overfill the blender. Make sure you remove the plastic center piece from the blender lid before blending and cover with a folded towel and your hand while blending. The hot liquid will expand and the soup will explode all over your kitchen otherwise.

Garnish the soup with the toasted pumpkin seeds.

Quick Roasted Beet Salad

- Dairy-Free Adaptable

- Grain-Free

- Vegetarian

I came up with this recipe out of sheer panic. My husband had called to say he had run into an old friend and was bringing him home for a home-cooked meal prepared by his "gourmet" wife. It had been a busy day working on my first book, Simply . . . Gluten-free Desserts, and I was looking forward to just heating up a rotisserie chicken that I had just picked up at the market, serving it with a green salad, and calling it dinner.

I rummaged through my pantry and found two cans of beets. How they got there I did not know, but I figured with a little roasting I could transform them. I cut the chicken into pieces and heated it with some quartered lemons and sprigs of rosemary. I added this quick beet salad, a quinoa pilaf (page 107), and pulled out one of the desserts I had in my refrigerator from recipe testing. Our guest left well-fed and happy and I breathed a huge sigh of relief.

The goat cheese, while very "gourmet," is not essential if dairy is a problem or if you don't normally stock it in your pantry.

Two 14.5-ounce cans standard cut beets (cut in chunks not sliced) rinsed, drained, and patted dry
½ cup plus 1 tablespoon olive oil
Kosher or fine sea salt
Freshly ground black pepper
1 cup walnuts

Finely grated zest and juice of 1 large or 2 small oranges
1 tablespoon balsamic vinegar
½ tablespoon honey
4 cups arugula (or other salad greens)
4 ounces goat cheese (optional)

Preheat the oven to 450 degrees.

Put the beets in a baking dish, drizzle with 1 tablespoon of the olive oil, and sprinkle with salt and pepper. Put the walnuts on a rimmed baking sheet. Bake

the beets for 15 minutes, stirring once or twice. Put the walnuts in the oven with the beets and toast for 5 minutes, or until the nuts are fragrant.

While the beets and walnuts are roasting, make the dressing. Whisk the orange zest, juice, balsamic vinegar, honey, and about ½ teaspoon of salt and ¼ teaspoon of pepper together. Continue whisking while you drizzle in the olive oil. Taste and adjust seasoning with additional salt and pepper, if needed.

When the beets and walnuts are done remove from the oven. Just before serving, toss the arugula with the dressing and divide it among four individual salad plates. Top with the beets and walnuts. Crumble the goat cheese on top if using. Serve immediately.

Pantry Salad

- Dairy-Free

- Vegetarian

Serves 10 to 12

This is the kind of salad I throw together after arriving home from a trip and to a refrigerator that was emptied prior to leaving. The beauty of this recipe is you can change it up to suit your tastes and what's in the pantry.

Giardiniera is a spicy pickled vegetable mixture usually found in the condiment aisle of the supermarket or in Italian specialty food stores. It typically contains carrots, onions, celery, cauliflower, and peppers. I love the bite it adds to this salad, and the vegetables, while still crisp, have a texture more suitable with the canned beans than raw vegetables. This salad can be eaten immediately, but it also improves with age and can be stored, covered, in the refrigerator for up to 4 days.

One 15-ounce can black beans, rinsed and drained

One 15-ounce can red kidney beans, rinsed and drained

One 15-ounce can chickpeas, rinsed and drained

One 16-ounce bottle giardiniera, drained

1 small red onion, finely chopped

1 tablespoon red wine vinegar

2 tablespoons olive oil

1/2 teaspoon freshly ground black pepper

Kosher or fine sea salt (optional)

Combine the drained and rinsed canned beans in a large bowl. Cut any large pieces of giardiniera into smaller bite-size pieces and add to the beans along with the onion.

In a small bowl, whisk together the vinegar, olive oil, and black pepper. Add to the beans and toss to coat. Taste and add salt, if needed. Serve immediately, or cover and refrigerate until ready to serve.

Baked Risotto

While not a classic risotto, this is so simple to prepare and just as delicious. The risotto is baked in the oven thus forgoing all the stovetop stirring.

Think of this recipe as a canvas to which you can add your own creativity. Stir in re-constituted dried mushrooms, frozen peas, cooked chicken—the only limit to the possibilities is your imagination and what you have on hand in your kitchen. Roast a pan of precut butternut squash along with a little olive oil, salt, and pepper while the risotto is baking. Stir it into the rice at the last minute for a lovely butternut squash risotto.

• Vegetarian Adaptable

Serves 4 to 6

---

2 tablespoons olive oil

1 medium white onion, finely chopped (about ½ cup)

1½ cups arborio rice

½ cup dry white wine

4¼ cups gluten-free chicken (or vegetable) stock, warmed

1 teaspoon kosher or fine sea salt

½ teaspoon freshly ground black pepper

½ cup Parmesan cheese, plus more for serving

3 tablespoons cold, unsalted butter, cut into pieces

Preheat the oven to 400 degrees. Heat the olive oil in a large ovenproof saucepan or Dutch oven with a lid over medium-high heat. Add the onion and sauté until tender, about 5 minutes. Add the rice, stir to coat with the oil, and cook for 1 minute. Stir in the wine and cook until it has completely evaporated, 1 to 2 minutes. Stir in 3 cups of the chicken broth, salt, and pepper and bring to a simmer, cover the pan, and bake, stirring once halfway through cooking time, until the rice is tender and the liquid is absorbed, 25 to 30 minutes.

Remove the rice from the oven and vigorously stir in the remaining 1¼ cups of warm chicken stock, then add the cheese and butter, stirring until creamy. Taste the risotto and add more salt and pepper if needed.

Grate over some additional Parmesan cheese, if desired, and serve.

Bean and Veggie Chili

- Dairy-Free

- Vegetarian/
Vegan

This is the recipe you need when you have a crowd of hungry people to feed and limited time and budget. A great vegetarian main dish on its own, this is also a perfect side for a backyard barbecue or to take to a potluck dinner. And as with most chili recipes, the leftovers just keep getting better and better. I make up a whole batch even if I am only feeding my husband and me; we eat it all week long and it also freezes well.

I frequently make this recipe with fresh red bell peppers that I sauté with the onions but for pantry-raid emergencies, jarred roasted red peppers work just as well.

2 tablespoons olive oil
1 large white onion, roughly
   chopped
Kosher or fine sea salt
Freshly ground black pepper
2 garlic cloves, minced
12 ounces jarred, roasted red
   bell peppers, drained,
   patted dry, and cut into large
   dice

Three 30-ounce cans kidney
   beans, rinsed and drained
Two 30-ounce cans diced
   tomatoes with their juices
½ cup gluten-free, mild taco
   sauce (such as Ortega)
½ cup A.1. Steak Sauce
1 to 3 tablespoons chili powder
   depending on the amount of
   heat you like

Heat the olive oil in a large, heavy stockpot over medium-high heat. Add the onion and cook for about 5 minutes, stirring occasionally, until the onion starts to get translucent. Season with a large pinch of salt and black pepper. Add the garlic and cook for another 1 to 2 minutes until the garlic has softened but is not browned.

Add the roasted red bell peppers, beans, tomatoes (including the juice), taco sauce, A.1. Sauce, and 1 tablespoon chili powder. (You can add more later depend-

ing on your desired heat level.) Stir well to combine. Bring to almost boiling, then reduce the heat and simmer, covered, for about 30 minutes, or until the liquid has reduced and the chili is thick, stirring every once in a while. Taste and adjust the seasoning with more salt, black pepper, or chili powder, if needed.

The chili can be made a day or two ahead, and gets better as time goes by.

Note: If you prefer to use fresh bell peppers, substitute two that have been seeded and chopped for the jar of peppers and add with the onion.

Sausage, Artichoke, and Olive Pasta

• Dairy-Free

I once invited about fifteen people to my house for some food after a fancy art show where the wine was free-flowing but the food on the skimpy side. It wasn't until I walked into the kitchen that I realized I had no plan for what to prepare. Fortunately there are some things I always have on hand that can be thrown together in a flash. This pasta is a weeknight staple at our house and thankfully a crowd-pleaser. (I might add that on the night of the art show I whipped this up in high heels and a cocktail dress.)

1 pound gluten-free pasta

2 tablespoons olive oil

1 medium onion, chopped

2 garlic cloves, minced

1 pound chicken sausage, sliced

One 14-ounce can quartered artichoke hearts in water, drained

One 14.5-ounce can diced tomatoes with their juices

1 tablespoon tomato paste

2 teaspoons dried Italian seasoning

1 teaspoon kosher or fine sea salt

1/2 teaspoon freshly ground black pepper

1/4 teaspoon crushed red pepper flakes

1 cup black pitted olives (preferably kalamata but any kind will do)

Parmesan cheese for serving (optional)

Cook the pasta in a large pot of salted boiling water according to the package directions.

While the pasta is cooking, make the sauce. Heat the olive oil in a large skillet over medium-high heat. Add the onion and cook until it starts to soften, about 3 minutes. Add the garlic and cook for another minute. Add the sliced sausage and brown. Add the artichoke hearts and cook for a minute or two. Add the tomatoes with their juice, the tomato paste, Italian seasoning, salt, black

pepper, and red pepper flakes. Cook, stirring occasionally, until most of the liquid has evaporated, 10 to 15 minutes. Add the olives and cook until heated through.

When the pasta is al dente, ladle out about ¼ cup of the pasta cooking liquid and add it to the sauce. Drain the pasta and return it to the hot pot. Add the sauce to the pasta and toss to coat. Taste and add additional salt and pepper, if needed.

Serve with or without grated Parmesan cheese.

Salmon Cakes

- Dairy-Free

Serves 4

This is what I call a rummage recipe—I rummaged through my pantry, tossed what I found together, and hoped for the best. All I was hoping for was to stave off starvation; I wasn't looking for a rave review, but get one I did. My husband loved it! I prefer to let him think that much thought and planning went into this recipe rather than tell him it was just lucky happenstance.

One 14.75-ounce can salmon (do not drain)
1½ cups gluten-free, panko-style bread crumbs
3 large eggs, lightly beaten
2 heaping teaspoons Old Bay Seasoning

One 2.25-ounce can sliced black olives, drained
1 cup frozen corn kernels, thawed
3 scallions, finely chopped
3 tablespoons olive or grapeseed oil

In a large mixing bowl, flake the salmon with a fork. Add the bread crumbs, eggs, Old Bay Seasoning, olives, corn, and scallions. Mix well and form into 8 patties, each about ½ inch thick, compacting firmly.

Heat the oil in a large skillet over medium-high heat. Fry the patties in batches (do not overcrowd the pan) for 3 to 4 minutes per side, or until nicely browned.

Dairy-Free Peanut Butter Fudge Sauce

• Dairy-Free

Makes enough sauce for 4 to 6 sundaes

I find that if I make something fabulous for dessert, dinner can be very basic and no one complains. The easiest pantry dessert is of course a dish of ice cream, but to make it really special it needs something to dress it up.

One of the things I love about canned coconut milk is that it sits in my pantry waiting for me, no refrigeration required. Mixing with some dairy-free chocolate chips and peanut butter turns that coconut milk into a decadent, rich, fudgy sauce with no coconut flavor.

Top some dairy-free ice cream with this sauce and perhaps a sprinkling of chopped, salty peanuts and you have created a fabulous, company-worthy dessert in less than 5 minutes.

³⁄₄ cup coconut milk (shake the can well before measuring)	¹⁄₂ cup creamy peanut butter
³⁄₄ cup semisweet, dairy-free chocolate chips	3 tablespoons agave nectar or corn syrup
	1 teaspoon vanilla extract

Combine the coconut milk, chocolate chips, peanut butter, and agave nectar in a small saucepan over medium heat and cook, stirring occasionally, until everything is melted together, about 2 minutes. Stir in the vanilla extract and let the sauce cool slightly. Serve on scoops of regular or dairy-free ice cream; the sauce thickens as it cools.

Slow, Slow, Quick, Quick

QUICK COOKING DOES not always mean that the entire recipe will be done, start to finish, in half an hour. Sometimes it means minimal preparation but a long time spent in a slow cooker, oven, or refrigerator, which is actually easier and quicker.

These recipes are not ones that can be thrown together right before a meal, but they make dinner or entertaining simple, as the work is done largely ahead of time.

Eggs Benedict Strata

• Dairy-Free Adaptable

Eggs Benedict just scream out "brunch" to me, but honestly, who wants to spend time over a stove poaching eggs when there are people to chat with and fun to be had? My solution? Eggs Benedict Strata. While it may seem this recipe takes a long time to prepare since it needs to sit in the refrigerator overnight and spend an hour in the oven, in reality it only take a few moments of actual hands-on preparation. Plan ahead and make this the night before you want to serve it and then get ready to wow your guests. Stick it in the oven while you get on with making coffee, setting the table, or just going back to bed and catching a few more winks.

4 gluten-free English muffins, thawed, split, and toasted
8 ounces Canadian bacon
10 large eggs
1 teaspoon dry mustard powder
1 1/2 teaspoons kosher or fine sea salt
1/2 teaspoon freshly ground black pepper

1 teaspoon paprika
2 1/4 cups milk (regular or dairy-free)
1 tablespoon freshly squeezed lemon juice
1 or 2 dashes hot sauce
1/2 cup (1 stick) butter or dairy-free butter substitute, melted

The day before you plan to serve the strata, spray a 12 × 9-inch baking dish with nonstick cooking spray.

Cut the toasted English muffins into 1-inch chunks. Cut the Canadian bacon into 1-inch pieces. Layer half the Canadian bacon in the bottom of the prepared dish. Top with the English muffin chunks and then add the remaining Canadian bacon pieces.

Separate four of the eggs and put the yolks in an airtight container and refrigerate until it is time to make the hollandaise sauce. Put the egg whites in a

large mixing bowl with the remaining whole eggs, ½ teaspoon of the dry mustard, 1 teaspoon of the salt, the pepper, paprika, and milk. Whisk to combine. Pour the egg mixture over the muffin chunks and Canadian bacon in the baking dish, cover with plastic wrap, and refrigerate overnight (8 to 12 hours).

One hour and 10 minutes before you plan to serve, preheat the oven to 375 degrees and remove the strata from the refrigerator. Remove the plastic wrap and cover with aluminum foil. Bake for 40 minutes, remove the foil, and continue to bake for 20 minutes, or until the top is nicely browned and the strata is set. Let cool 5 minutes before serving.

While the strata is cooling make the hollandaise sauce. Put the reserved egg yolks in the blender along with the remaining ½ teaspoon dry mustard, remaining ½ teaspoon of salt, lemon juice, and hot sauce. Blend for 5 seconds. Remove the small plastic top from the blender lid and, with the blender running, slowly drizzle in the melted butter. Continue blending until all the butter has been incorporated. The sauce can be kept warm, if needed, by placing in a heatproof bowl over barely simmering water, making sure the bottom of the bowl is not touching the water. It takes so little time and effort to make the hollandaise I usually just whip it up while the strata is cooling. Put the sauce into a small serving bowl and serve with the strata.

Spicy Noodles

• Dairy-Free

• Vegetarian/
Vegan Adaptable

Serves 8 to 10

I wish I could take full credit for this recipe but, in fact, it comes from my good friend Jan Regan, who has made this her signature dish. I adapted the recipe to be gluten-free. I have even made versions of this dish nut-free by using sunflower butter in place of peanut butter and omitting the peanuts.

The dish needs to chill in the refrigerator for at least 4 hours for the flavors to meld, but it does not take long to prepare and makes a great potluck dish as it is easy to transport and everyone loves it.

1 pound gluten-free noodles (can use gluten-free spaghetti or rice sticks, either thick or thin)

¼ cup grapeseed or vegetable oil

½ cup sesame oil

1 tablespoon crushed red pepper flakes (more or less depending on how spicy you want it)

½ cup creamy or chunky peanut butter

6 tablespoons honey (to make vegan, substitute agave nectar)

5 tablespoons wheat-free, gluten-free soy sauce

2 bunches scallions, thinly sliced

½ bunch cilantro, chopped

Kosher or fine sea salt

Freshly ground black pepper

¼ cup sesame seeds or ¾ cup chopped salted peanuts or both

Break the noodles in half and cook according to the package directions. Drain and transfer to a large bowl.

In a medium saucepan, heat the oils. Add the red pepper flakes and cook for 1 minute. Add the peanut butter, honey, and soy sauce. Cook, stirring, for a minute to combine and melt the peanut butter. Pour the mixture over the cooked noodles, reserve a couple tablespoons of the sliced scallions and cilantro for garnish, and add the rest to the noodles. Taste and season with salt and black pepper, if desired. Toss well and refrigerate, covered, for at least 4 hours or overnight.

Just prior to serving, garnish with the reserved sliced scallions and chopped cilantro and sprinkle with the sesame seeds or chopped peanuts or both.

Brined Pork Chops with Spicy Pear Chutney

• Dairy-Free

Many years ago the pork industry responded to consumer demand for leaner meat and started breeding pigs with less fat. They achieved the result of leaner cuts of pork, but also ended up with fairly tasteless meat. The solution to this flaw is brining.

Left to languish in a salty solution for many hours, the pork chops in this recipe absorb flavor and cook quickly and beautifully. With brining you can take the cheapest pork chop in the supermarket and turn it into a restaurant-quality meal.

I have updated the classic pork chop and applesauce dinner by taking away the bland, baby food-like applesauce and replacing it with a spicy pear chutney that can be whipped up in just a little bit more time than it takes to cook the pork chops.

BRINED PORK CHOPS
4 cups water
1/4 cup kosher salt
1/4 cup firmly packed brown sugar
1 teaspoon freshly ground black
    pepper
1 tablespoon apple cider vinegar
6 pork chops (about 3/4 inch thick)
1/2 white onion, sliced
2 or 3 springs fresh sage
Olive oil for brushing the pork chops

SPICY PEAR CHUTNEY
1 tablespoon olive oil
1/2 medium red onion, minced

1/2 cup dried cranberries
1/4 cup granulated sugar
1 tablespoon apple cider vinegar
1 tablespoon freshly squeezed
    lemon juice
1 teaspoon kosher or sea salt
1/2 teaspoon freshly ground black
    pepper
1/4 to 1/2 teaspoon hot red pepper
    flakes (depending on how
    spicy you want it)
3 fresh pears, peeled, cored, and
    chopped

To brine the pork chops, combine 1 cup water with the salt, brown sugar, and pepper in a small saucepan. Heat, stirring, until the salt and sugar dissolve. Add 3 cups of cold water and let the mixture cool. Stir in the apple cider vinegar. Pour the mixture into a glass baking dish or large freezer-weight plastic storage bag. Add the pork chops, onions, and sage. Refrigerate for 1 to 12 hours (but not more than 12 hours); even a little bit of brining is better than none.

To make the chutney, place a large saucepan over medium heat. Add the olive oil and minced red onion and cook for 2 or 3 minutes until the onion starts to soften. Add the dried cranberries and cook for 5 minutes more. Stir in the sugar, vinegar, lemon juice, salt, black pepper, red pepper flakes, and pears and combine well. Reduce the heat to low and simmer for 5 to 10 minutes, or until the pears and cranberries have softened but the pears still retain their shape. If the mixture is too liquid, increase the heat and cook until most of the liquid has evaporated. Serve warm.

When ready to cook, take the pork chops out of the refrigerator and rinse them well under cold running water. Pat dry with paper towels and set the chops aside for about 5 minutes before cooking.

Heat a grill pan or skillet over medium-high heat. Brush the pork chops with olive oil and cook for 4 minutes per side (more or less depending on the thickness of the pork chops). Remove from the pan, brush the tops with a little more olive oil, and let rest for 5 minutes before serving.

Chicken Adobo

• Dairy-Free

Serves 6

Since my early formative years were spent in the Philippines, I have always had a fondness for Filipino food. This is a slow cooker version of Chicken Adobo. If you have time, throw all the ingredients into a large food storage bag and let marinate in the refrigerator overnight; the flavor will be even more intense. I use skinless, bone-in chicken thighs because I think they have more flavor, but you can use any chicken parts you want, bone-in or boneless, though I do recommend taking the skin off. Serve the chicken with rice to soak up the flavorful juices.

3 to 4 pounds chicken pieces
1 medium onion, halved and
    thinly sliced
1/2 cup apple cider vinegar
1/2 cup gluten-free soy sauce
3 bay leaves

6 garlic cloves, crushed
1 tablespoon brown sugar
1 teaspoon kosher or fine sea salt
1 1/2 teaspoons freshly ground
    black pepper
Cooked rice for serving

Combine all the ingredients in a 4-quart slow cooker and let sit for 15 minutes to come to room temperature. Cook on high for 3 to 4 hours or on low for 5 to 6 hours; the meat should be very tender and falling off the bone. Remove and discard the bay leaves. Serve hot with rice.

South-of-the-Border Short Ribs

⟨∿∿∿∿∿∿∿∿∿∿∿∿∿∿∿∿∿⟩

Short ribs are a flavorful cut of meat that really benefits from long, slow cooking. The slow cooker is the perfect vessel for making fall-off-the-bone-tender short ribs with very little effort. Ask the butcher for extra-lean short ribs and they won't create much fat in the sauce.

For stress-free entertaining, start with a simple salad, then place the ribs on smashed potatoes, polenta, or rice, and be ready to receive raves.

• Dairy-Free

Serves 6

---

1 teaspoon kosher or fine sea salt
½ teaspoon freshly ground black
    pepper
2 teaspoons chili powder
3 to 4 pounds extra-lean bone-in beef
    short ribs (plan on 2 per person)
3 small leeks, white and light
    green parts, sliced ¼ inch thick
3 large sweet potatoes, peeled
    and cut into 2-inch chunks

1¼ cups mango nectar
½ cup gluten-free beef stock
¼ cup tequila
1 tablespoon cornstarch or
    arrowroot powder
3 scallions, thinly sliced
Dairy-Free, Ranch-Style
    Smashed Potatoes
    (page 36), polenta, or rice
    for serving

Mix the salt, pepper, and chili powder together in a small bowl. Sprinkle the mixture over the short ribs. Place the short ribs in a 6-quart slow cooker and add the leeks and sweet potatoes.

Combine 1 cup mango nectar with the beef stock and tequila and pour over the ribs and vegetables. Cook on low for 7 to 9 hours.

Remove the ribs and vegetables from the slow cooker and place in a serving dish. Combine the cornstarch with the remaining ¼ cup mango nectar. Pour the sauce into a saucepan, skim off any visible fat, and bring to a boil. Add the mango-cornstarch mixture and boil, stirring constantly, for 1 minute, or until the sauce has thickened. Pour the sauce over the ribs and vegetables. Garnish with the sliced scallions. Serve with smashed potatoes, polenta, or rice.

Pork Roast with Apple Gravy

• Dairy-Free

Serves 8

Pork and apples have a natural affinity for one another and this easy roast marries the two quite well. Ask your butcher to remove the excess fat from the pork loin roast or simply trim it off yourself. If you really don't want to go to any additional bother, you could skip the browning process but your roast won't look as pretty.

I still have the slow cooker I got for a wedding present back in the '70s. With that older model it takes about 10 hours for the roast to fully cook, but with my newer one it only takes 7 to 8 hours.

2 teaspoons kosher or fine sea salt
1 teaspoon freshly ground black
    pepper
1 teaspoon garlic powder
One 4-pound pork loin roast,
    trimmed of excess fat

4 apples, peeled, cored, and each
    cut into 6 wedges
½ cup apple juice
3 tablespoons maple syrup

Preheat the oven to 450 degrees.

Combine the salt, pepper, and garlic powder in a small bowl. Rub the mixture all over the pork roast. Place the roast in a roasting pan, fat side up, and roast in the oven for 15 minutes, or until the top starts to brown.

Place the apples in the bottom of a 6-quart slow cooker and place the roast on top. Combine the apple juice and maple syrup and pour over the pork. Cook on low for 7 to 8 hours (unless you have a really old slow cooker, then increase the time to 9 to 10 hours). The internal temperature of the roast should register 155 degrees.

When the roast is done, transfer it to a serving platter. Using a potato masher, mash the apples into the sauce until you have a thick gravy. Slice the roast and spoon the apple gravy over the top.

Wine- and Rosemary-Braised Lamb Shanks with White Bean Mash

• Dairy-Free

This is an elegant, company-worthy meal that is so simple it is almost embarrassing. It is the ultimate slow, slow, quick, quick meal. The lamb shanks cook in the slow cooker for 10 to 12 hours, and the white bean mash takes about 3 minutes to make.

WINE- AND ROSEMARY-BRAISED LAMB SHANKS

1 large onion, roughly chopped

6 garlic cloves, peeled and smashed

4 to 5 sprigs of fresh rosemary

1/2 cup dry red wine

2 tablespoons Dijon mustard

2 teaspoons kosher or fine sea salt

1 teaspoon freshly ground black pepper

6 lamb foreshanks, about 1 pound each

Finely grated zest and juice of 1 lemon

1 tablespoon cornstarch or arrowroot powder

1/4 cup water

2 tablespoons cold unsalted butter or nondairy butter substitute

WHITE BEAN MASH

1/4 cup olive oil

1 garlic clove, peeled and lightly smashed

1 sprig fresh rosemary

3 cans white beans, drained and rinsed

Kosher or fine sea salt

Freshly ground black pepper

For the lamb shanks, place the onion, garlic, and rosemary sprigs in the bottom of a 6-quart slow cooker. In a small bowl, combine the wine, mustard, salt, and pepper. Place the lamb shanks in the slow cooker and pour the wine

mixture over the top. Add the lemon zest and juice. Cook on low for 10 to 12 hours.

For the white bean mash, heat the olive oil in a medium saucepan over medium heat. Add the garlic clove and rosemary sprig. Cook until fragrant and they both start to brown lightly, about 30 seconds. Remove and discard the garlic and rosemary with a slotted spoon or tongs. Add the white beans to the oil and cook, stirring, until heated through, about 3 minutes. Mash the beans with a potato masher or the back of a spoon and season to taste with salt and pepper.

When the lamb is done, remove the shanks from the slow cooker and place in a serving bowl. Strain the sauce into a saucepan and bring to a boil on the stovetop. Combine the cornstarch with water and mix well. Add the cornstarch mixture to the boiling sauce and cook for 1 minute, or until the sauce has thickened. Whisk in the cold butter or nondairy butter substitute and pour the sauce over the shanks. Serve over white bean mash.

Many Thanks

I am so grateful that I have so many wonderful people in my life to thank. There is no way I could have written this cookbook, given my hectic schedule, without the support and help of my family and friends.

My husband, Thom, has been my most stable pillar of support for more years than I care to mention in public. He is always there for me, but when crunch time came at the end of this process he really stepped up to the plate, taking care of not only many daily chores but also me. I am so grateful for his help and encouragement but mostly I am just grateful for his existence.

My children, Colin and Dustin, have grown up to be fine upstanding men and are now paying me back in spades for helping them grow up by being there for whatever I need, small or big. I cannot express in words how proud I am of them. I am also grateful for the gorgeous grandchildren they have brought into my life.

Angie Moore is the very definition of the word "friend." She offered her help and support unconditionally and took things off my plate so that I could make the time to concentrate on writing this book.

My blog readers are, as always, a constant source of inspiration. They have become my virtual cheerleaders as I foray into the world as a cookbook author. The comments on my blog and e-mails I receive from my readers never fail to put a smile on my face and perk me up.

I doubt that all editors are as easy to work with as mine at Thomas Dunne Books, Peter Joseph. He not only brought me into this world of cookbook writing

but also nurtured and encouraged me along the way. I will always be grateful for his guidance and support.

My agent, Laurie Jessup, is so much more than an agent; she is a friend. I am thankful for her belief in me and for her help and guidance as I learn to navigate these new waters.

Index

A.1 Steak Sauce, 5
adobo
    Chicken Adobo, 192
agave nectar, 9
All-American Meat Loaf Dinner, 33
almond flour, 3
    Mini Almond Orange Cakes, 117
almond milk, 3
almonds
    Almond-Crusted Chicken Piccata,
        105
Almost Instant Nutella Mousse, 130
apple cider vinegar, 9
apples
    in muffins, 21
    Pork Roast with Apple Gravy, 194
    Quick "Baked" Apples, 82
apricots, 5
arborio rice, 8
arrowroot, 5
artichoke
    Sausage, Artichoke, and Olive Pasta,
        180
arugula
    Arugula Salad, 108
    Pear and Arugula Salad, 70
Asian-Inspired Salmon and Rice Supper,
    44
Asian markets
    buying ingredients at, 17
Asian Noodles and Meat Sauce, 85
Asian Ragu Supper, 83
asparagus
    Roasted Asparagus, 122
Authentic Foods brand, 4, 24

bacon
    Rustic Salad, 42
Baked Risotto, 177
Baked Tomatoes, 65
baking powder, 3
    corn-free, 3
baking soda, 4
balsamic vinegar, 9
    Balsamic Strawberries with Mascarpone
        Cream, 99
    Oven-Roasted Balsamic Onion Green Beans,
        150
bananas
    Banana-Date Muffins, 164
    in muffins, 21
    Piña Colada Smoothie, 161
bars
    Vegan Breakfast Bars, 166
basic breads, 18–22
basmati rice
    Spiced Basmati Rice with Cashews, 75
bay leaves, 5
beans
    Bean and Veggie Chili, 178
    canned, 4
    Pantry Salad, 176
    See also black beans; green beans; white
        beans
Béarnaise Sauce, 123
beef
    Roast Beef Dinner, 152
    Roasted Beef Tenderloin with Red Onion
        Gravy, 154
beef stock
    gluten-free, 6

beets
    Quick Roasted Beet Salad, 174
berries
    Instant Berry Frozen Yogurt, 66
    mixed, frozen, 6
biscuit mix
    basic, 18
    Whole Grain Pancake and Biscuit Mix, 24
biscuits
    basic, 22
    Buttermilk Biscuits, 23
    drop, 22
    rolled, 22
    variations of, 23
    Whole Grain Biscuits, 28
bites
    Glazed Chorizo Bites, 114
black beans
    Black Bean Blender Soup, 172
    Quick Black Beans, 135
Black Forest Trifle, 158
black pepper, 5
blenders, 12
    Black Bean Blender Soup, 172
    Easy Blender Béarnaise Sauce, 123
Blitzed Brownies, 43
blueberries
    Blueberry Fool, 109
    in muffins, 21
bread crumbs
    gluten-free, panko-style, 6–7
breads
    gluten-free, 7
    Rustic Salad, 42
    Whole Grain Muffins and Quick Breads,
        26
breakfasts, 160–67
    Breakfast Quesadilla, 162
    getting family to eat, 160
    Vegan Breakfast Bars, 166
Brined Pork Chops with Spicy Pear Chutney,
    190
brining, 190
Broccoli with Garlic Chips, 37
brownies
    Blitzed Brownies, 43

brown rice, 8
    Brown Rice with Edamame, 47
brown rice flour, 4
brown sugar, 8
brussels sprouts
    Roasted Brussels Sprouts, 156
burgers
    Falafel Burgers, 90
    Greek Burgers, 57
    Greek Burgers and Fries Supper, 55
butter
    Roasted Corn with Chili-Lime Butter,
        141
Buttermilk Biscuits, 23

cabbage
    Creamy Coleslaw, 142
cake mixes
    gluten-free, 6
cakes
    Mini Almond Orange Cakes, 117
    Salmon Cakes, 182
canned goods, 4
carrots
    Creamy Coleslaw, 142
    Glazed Carrots, 157
    Thai Carrot and Cucumber Salad, 86
cashews
    Spiced Basmati Rice with Cashews, 75
cayenne pepper, 5
Cheater's Rice Pudding, 61
cheddar cheese
    Shepherd's Pie, 79
cheese
    in muffins, 21
    Pistachio-Cranberry-Goat Cheese–Stuffed
        Pork Tenderloin, 127
    Quick Mac and Cheese, 64
    See also cheddar cheese; feta cheese; goat
        cheese
cheesecake
    Cookies and Cream No-Bake Cheesecakes,
        143
cherries, 5
    Black Forest Trifle, 158
    Hot Cherry Sundaes, 71

chicken
    Almond-Crusted Chicken Piccata, 105
    Chicken Adobo, 192
    Oven-Fried Chicken, 139
    Polenta Potpies, 69
    rotisserie, 12
chicken stock
    gluten-free, 6
chickpeas
    Falafel Burgers, 90
chili
    Bean and Veggie Chili, 178
chilies
    canned, mild, 4
    in muffins, 21
chili garlic paste, 5
chili powder, 5
    Roasted Corn with Chili-Lime Butter, 141
chipotle
    in adobo sauce, 4–5
    Chipotle Potato Salad, 140
chocolate, 5, 119
    Chocolate-Strawberry Fool, 124
    Dairy-Free Chocolate Ganache with Fruit, 38
chops
    Brined Pork Chops with Spicy Pear Chutney, 190
chorizo
    Glazed Chorizo Bites, 114
Christmas Day Dinner, 152
chutney
    Brined Pork Chops with Spicy Pear Chutney, 190
Cinco de Mayo Feast, 131
cinnamon, 5
    in muffins, 21
Client Dinner, 103
cloves, 5
cocktail parties, 110
coconut
    Dairy-Free Coconut Pie, 136
coconut milk, 4, 183
coconut sugar, 9
cod
    Potato- and Herb-Crusted Cod, 96

coleslaw
    Creamy, 142
comfort food
    Cottage Comfort Supper, 77
    Quick Comfort Supper, 62
condiments, 5
confectioners' sugar, 8
cooker, slow, 12
Cookies and Cream No-Bake Cheesecakes, 143
cooking
    organization in, 11
    in oven, 13
    restaurant practices, 11–12
    reviewing recipes before starting, 12
cooking spray, 7
coriander, 5
corn
    frozen, 6
    Roasted Corn with Chili-Lime Butter, 141
corn allergy, 5, 9
corn-free baking powder, 3
Cornish Game Hens
    Roasted, 146
cornstarch, 5
Cottage Comfort Supper, 77
cottage pie. *See* Shepherd's Pie
crackers
    gluten-free, graham-style, 6
cranberries, 5
    Cranberry Gravy, 148
    in muffins, 21
    Pistachio-Cranberry-Goat Cheese–Stuffed Pork Tenderloin, 127
    Spinach Salad with Mushrooms, Red Onions, and Cranberries, 81
cream
    Balsamic Strawberries with Mascarpone Cream, 99
    Cookies and Cream No-Bake Cheesecakes, 143
Creamy Coleslaw, 142
Creamy Tahini Sauce, 91
cross contamination, 7
crumbs
    gluten-free, graham-style, 6

cucumbers
  Quick Tzatziki Sauce, 58
  Thai Carrot and Cucumber Salad, 86
cumin, 5
cups
  Egg Florentine Cups, 165
curry, 72
  Curry in a Hurry Supper, 72
  Vegetable Curry, 74
curry powder, 5

Dairy-Free Adaptable Recipes
  All-American Meat Loaf Dinner, 33
  Banana-Date Muffins, 164
  Black Bean Blender Soup, 172
  Creamy Tahini Sauce, 91
  Egg Florentine Cups, 165
  Eggs Benedict Strata, 187
  Pistachio-Spinach Pesto, 171
  Quick Roasted Beet Salad, 174
  Whole Grain Biscuits, 28
  Whole Grain Muffins and Quick Breads, 26
  Whole Grain Pancakes, 25
  Whole Grain Quick Breads, 26
Dairy-Free Recipes
  Bean and Veggie Chili, 178
  Breakfast Quesadilla, 162
  Brined Pork Chops with Spicy Pear Chutney,
    190
  Chicken Adobo, 192
  Dairy-Free, Ranch-Style Smashed Potatoes,
    36
  Dairy-Free Chocolate Ganache with Fruit,
    38
  Dairy-Free Coconut Pie, 136
  Dairy-Free Mango Lassis, 76
  Dairy-Free Peanut Butter Fudge Sauce, 183
  Mexican Pumpkin Soup, 173
  Pantry Salad, 176
  Pork Roast with Apple Gravy, 194
  Salmon Cakes, 182
  Sausage, Artichoke, and Olive Pasta, 180
  South-of-the-Border Short Ribs, 193
  Spicy Noodles, 189
  Vegan Breakfast Bars, 166
  Whole Grain Overnight Porridge, 163

Whole Grain Pancake and Biscuit Mix, 24
Wine- and Rosemary-Braised Lamb Shanks
  with White Bean Mash, 195
Date Night Dinner, 118
dates, 5
  Banana-Date Muffins, 164
dinners
  All-American Meat Loaf Dinner, 33
  Client Dinner, 103
  Date Night Dinner, 118
  In-Laws for Dinner, 125
  Middle Eastern Dinner, 88
  Pie for Dinner, 67
  Quick Thanksgiving Dinner, 144
  Roast Beef Dinner, 152
  Rustic Elegance Dinner, 39
  See also suppers
dip
  Roasted Shrimp with Romesco Dip, 116
dressing
  Skillet Dressing, 147
dumplings, 23, 29

Easy Blender Béarnaise Sauce, 123
Easy Mexican Rice, 134
edamame
  Brown Rice with Edamame, 47
eggs
  Béarnaise Sauce, 123
  Egg Florentine Cups, 165
  Eggs Benedict Strata, 187
  Yorkshire Puddings, 155
Enchilada Lasagna, 51
English muffins
  gluten-free, 7
entertaining, 102–58
  tips for making it easy, 102
equipment, 12
extracts, 6
extra-virgin olive oil, 8

Falafel Burgers, 90
family meals, 32, 160
feasts
  Cinco de Mayo Feast, 131
  Weeknight Mexican Fiesta, 49

feta cheese
  Greek Burgers, 57
  Greek Salad, 60
Filet Mignon, Steakhouse, 121
Filipino food, 192
finger method for testing doneness of steaks, 121
fish. *See* cod; salmon; tuna
fish sauce, 5
flour blends
  gluten-free, preparing one's own, 16
  Sweet Rice Flour Blend, 8
food processors, 12
Fool
  Blueberry Fool, 109
  Chocolate-Strawberry Fool, 124
fresh ingredients, 12
fries
  Greek Burgers and Fries Supper, 55
frozen fruits and vegetables, 6
fruit
  canned, 4
  Dairy-Free Chocolate Ganache with Fruit, 38
  dried, 5
  frozen, 6
  Vegan Breakfast Bars, 166
  washing, 11
fudge
  Dairy-Free Peanut Butter Fudge Sauce, 183

ganache
  Dairy-Free Chocolate Ganache with Fruit, 38
garlic
  Broccoli with Garlic Chips, 37
garlic powder, 5
giardiniera, 176
ginger, 5
Glazed Carrots, 157
Glazed Chorizo Bites, 114
Glazed Salmon, 46
gluten-free ingredients
  bread, 7
  bread crumbs, 6–7
  cake mixes, 6
  dried pasta, 5
  English muffins, 7

flour blends, 16
  graham-style crackers, 6
  stock, 6
gluten-free meals
  for entertaining guests, 102
glutinous rice flour. *See* sweet (glutinous) rice flour
goat cheese
  Pistachio-Cranberry-Goat Cheese–Stuffed Pork Tenderloin, 127
grain. *See* whole grains
Grain-Free Recipe
  Quick Roasted Beet Salad, 174
granulated sugar, 8
grapeseed oil, 8
graters
  microplane, 12
gravy
  Cranberry Gravy, 148
  Pork Roast with Apple Gravy, 194
  Roasted Beef Tenderloin with Red Onion Gravy, 154
Greek Burgers, 57
Greek Burgers and Fries Supper, 55
Greek Salad, 60
green beans
  Oven-Roasted Balsamic Onion Green Beans, 150
green salad, 129
ground lamb
  Greek Burgers, 57
ground sirloin
  Mini Meat Loaves, 35
  Shepherd's Pie, 79
guar gum, 9

ham
  Egg Florentine Cups, 165
health food stores
  buying ingredients at, 17
herbs and spices
  dried, 5–6
  Potato- and Herb-Crusted Cod, 96
hollandaise sauces, 187–88
Honey-Roasted Plums, 93
Hot Cherry Sundaes, 71

hot pepper sauce, 5
hot red pepper flakes, 5

ice cream, 7
ingredients
   fresh, 12
   where to buy, 17
In-Laws for Dinner, 125
Instant Berry Frozen Yogurt, 66
Italian seasoning, 5

jalapeño peppers, 4–5
jams, 5
jellies, 5

kalamata olives, 8
ketchup, 5
Kinnikinnick brand, 6–7
knives, 12
kosher salt, 8

lamb
   Greek Burgers, 57
   Wine- and Rosemary-Braised Lamb Shanks
      with White Bean Mash, 195
lasagna
   Enchilada Lasagna, 51
lassis
   Dairy-Free Mango Lassis, 76
Lazy Summer Afternoon Party, 137
Lemon-Roasted Fingerling Potatoes, 59
lettuce
   Simple Green Salad, 129
limes
   Roasted Corn with Chili-Lime Butter,
      141

macaroni
   Quick Mac and Cheese, 64
Manchego-Stuffed Peppers, 115
mango
   chunks, frozen, 6
   Dairy-Free Mango Lassis, 76
   Quick Mango Sticky Rice, 87
Maple Mashed Sweet Potatoes, 149
maple syrup, 9

marmalade
   Orange and Red Onion Salad, 53
mascarpone
   Balsamic Strawberries with Mascarpone
      Cream, 99
mash
   Maple Mashed Sweet Potatoes, 149
   Wine- and Rosemary-Braised Lamb Shanks
      with White Bean Mash, 195
mayonnaise
   Creamy Coleslaw, 142
   substitute, 7
measuring cups, 12
measuring spoons, 12
meat loaf
   All-American Meat Loaf Dinner, 33
   Mini Meat Loaves, 35
meat sauce
   Asian Noodles and Meat Sauce, 85
menu planning, 11
Mexican food
   Cinco de Mayo Feast, 131
   Easy Mexican Rice, 134
   Mexican Pumpkin Soup, 173
   Mexico City Broil, 133
   Weeknight Mexican Fiesta, 49
microwave oven, 12
Middle Eastern Dinner, 88
millet
   Whole Grain Overnight Porridge, 163
millet flour, 7
Mini Almond Orange Cakes, 117
Mini Meat Loaves, 35
Mini Yorkshire Puddings, 155
mint
   Smashed Minty Peas, 98
mise en place, 11–12
mixer (kitchen equipment), 12
mixes, 16–29
   Whole Grain Pancake and Biscuit Mix, 24
mousse
   Almost Instant Nutella Mousse, 130
   Pumpkin Mousse Pie, 151
muffins
   Banana-Date Muffins, 164
   basic, 20

English muffins, gluten-free, 7
variations of, by adding fruit, nuts, etc., 21
Whole Grain Muffins and Quick Breads,
   26
mushrooms
   dried, 6
   Spinach Salad with Mushrooms, Red Onions,
      and Cranberries, 81
mustard, 5

nonstick cooking spray, 7
noodles
   Asian Noodles and Meat Sauce, 85
   Spicy Noodles, 189
nutella
   Almost Instant Nutella Mousse, 130
nutmeg, 5
nuts, 8
   in muffins, 21

oats, 8
   Vegan Breakfast Bars, 166
oils, 8
olive oil, extra-virgin, 8
olives, 8
   black, sliced, 8
   Greek Salad, 60
   Sausage, Artichoke, and Olive Pasta, 180
onions
   baby, 6
   dried, 5
   Orange and Red Onion Salad, 53
   Oven-Roasted Balsamic Onion Green Beans,
      150
   Roasted Beef Tenderloin with Red Onion
      Gravy, 154
   Spinach Salad with Mushrooms, Red Onions,
      and Cranberries, 81
oranges
   in muffins, 21
   Orange and Red Onion Salad, 53
orange zest
   Mini Almond Orange Cakes, 117
oregano, 5
organization
   in cooking, 11

oven
   cooking in, 13
Oven-Fried Chicken, 139
Oven-Roasted Balsamic Onion Green Beans,
   150

palm sugar, 9
pancake and biscuit mixes
   basic, 18
   Whole Grain Pancake and Biscuit Mix, 24
pancakes
   basic, 19
   Whole Grain Pancakes, 25
pans, 12
pantry
   raiding, for quick meals, 170–83
   stocking with gluten-free ingredients, 3–9
Pantry Salad, 176
paprika, 5
parties
   Lazy Summer Afternoon Party, 137
   Tapas Party, 110
pasta
   gluten-free, dried, 5
   Ricotta and Tomato Pasta, 41
   Sausage, Artichoke, and Olive Pasta, 180
peanut butter, 8
   Dairy-Free Peanut Butter Fudge Sauce, 183
pears
   Brined Pork Chops with Spicy Pear Chutney,
      190
   Pear and Arugula Salad, 70
peas, 6
   frozen, 6
   Smashed Minty Peas, 98
pepper (spice), 5
peppers (vegetable)
   Manchego-Stuffed Peppers, 115
   See also jalapeño peppers; red peppers
pesto
   Pistachio-Spinach Pesto, 171
pickles
   Spicy Quick Pickles, 48
pie (dessert)
   Dairy-Free Coconut Pie, 136
   Pumpkin Mousse Pie, 151

pie (shape)
 Pie for Dinner, 67
 Polenta Potpies, 69
 Shepherd's Pie, 79
pilaf
 Quinoa Pilaf, 107
Piña Colada Smoothie, 161
pineapple
 Piña Colada Smoothie, 161
pistachio
 Pistachio-Cranberry-Goat Cheese–Stuffed
  Pork Tenderloin, 127
 Pistachio-Spinach Pesto, 171
plums
 Honey-Roasted Plums, 93
Polenta Potpies, 69
pork
 Asian Noodles and Meat Sauce, 85
 Brined Pork Chops with Spicy Pear Chutney,
  190
 lean and fat, 190
 Pistachio-Cranberry-Goat Cheese–Stuffed
  Pork Tenderloin, 127
 Pork Roast with Apple Gravy, 194
porridge
 Whole Grain Overnight Porridge, 163
potatoes
 Chipotle Potato Salad, 140
 Dairy-Free, Ranch-Style Smashed Potatoes,
  36
 instant mashed, for crusting fish, 94
 Lemon-Roasted Fingerling Potatoes,
  59
 Potato- and Herb-Crusted Cod, 96
 Shepherd's Pie, 79
 Skillet Potatoes, 97
 Spanish Tortilla, 113
potato starch, 8
potpies
 Polenta Potpies, 69
pots, 12
poultry seasoning, 5
precut salad greens and vegetables, 12,
 73
pudding mix
 Black Forest Trifle, 158

puddings
 Cheater's Rice Pudding, 61
 Mini Yorkshire Puddings, 155
pumpkin
 Mexican Pumpkin Soup, 173
 Pumpkin Mousse Pie, 151

quesadilla
 Breakfast, 162
Quick "Baked" Apples, 82
Quick Black Beans, 135
Quick Black Forest Trifle, 158
quick breads
 basic, 20
Quick Comfort Supper, 62
quick-cooking strategies, 11–13
 preparation for (slow, slow, quick, quick),
  186
Quick Macaroni and Cheese, 64
Quick Mango Sticky Rice, 87
Quick Roasted Beet Salad, 174
Quick Thanksgiving Dinner, 144
Quick Tzatziki Sauce, 58
quinoa, 8
 Quinoa Pilaf, 107
 Quinoa Tabbouleh, 92
 Whole Grain Overnight Porridge, 163

ragu
 Asian Ragu Supper, 83
ranch-style
 Dairy-Free, Ranch-Style Smashed Potatoes,
  36
raspberries
 frozen, 6
raw sugar, 8
recipes
 reviewing, before starting, 12
red onions
 Orange and Red Onion Salad, 53
 Roasted Beef Tenderloin with Red Onion
  Gravy, 154
 Spinach Salad with Mushrooms, Red Onions,
  and Cranberries, 81
red peppers
 jarred roasted, 7

red vinegar, 9
Regan, Jan, 189
restaurants
    cooking strategies of, 11–12
rice, 8
    Asian-Inspired Salmon and Rice Supper, 44
    Baked Risotto, 177
    Brown Rice with Edamame, 47
    Cheater's Rice Pudding, 61
    Easy Mexican Rice, 134
    Quick Mango Sticky Rice, 87
    Spiced Basmati Rice with Cashews, 75
    Sweet Rice Flour Blend, 8
rice sticks or vermicelli
    Asian Noodles and Meat Sauce, 85
rice vinegar, 9
Ricotta and Tomato Pasta, 41
risotto
    Baked, 177
roast
    Pork Roast with Apple Gravy, 194
    Roast Beef Dinner, 152
Roasted Asparagus, 122
Roasted Beef Tenderloin with Red Onion
    Gravy, 154
Roasted Brussels Sprouts, 156
Roasted Cornish Game Hens, 146
Roasted Corn with Chili-Lime Butter, 141
Roasted Shrimp with Romesco Dip, 116
Roasted Sweet Potato Wedges, 128
romance foods, 119
romesco
    Roasted Shrimp with Romesco Dip, 116
rosemary, 5
    Wine- and Rosemary-Braised Lamb Shanks
      with White Bean Mash, 195
rotisserie chicken, 12
Rustic Elegance Dinner, 39
Rustic Salad, 42

sage, 5
salad dressing, 9
salad greens, preprepped, 12
salads
    Arugula Salad, 108
    Chipotle Potato Salad, 140

Greek Salad, 60
Orange and Red Onion Salad, 53
Pantry Salad, 176
Pear and Arugula Salad, 70
Quick Roasted Beet Salad, 174
Rustic Salad, 42
Simple Green Salad, 129
Spinach Salad with Mushrooms, Red Onions,
    and Cranberries, 81
Thai Carrot and Cucumber Salad, 86
salmon
    Asian-Inspired Salmon and Rice Supper, 44
    Glazed Salmon, 46
    Salmon Cakes, 182
salsa
    jarred, 5
salt, 8
Sangaritas, 112
San Marzano tomatoes, 4
sauces, 5
    Creamy Tahini Sauce, 91
    Dairy-Free Peanut Butter Fudge Sauce,
      183
    Easy Blender Béarnaise Sauce, 123
    Quick Tzatziki Sauce, 58
Sausage, Artichoke, and Olive Pasta, 180
scallions
    Falafel Burgers, 90
sea salt, 8
seeds, 8
sesame oil, 8
Shepherd's Pie, 79
sherry vinegar, 9
shopping for food, 11
shortcakes, 23, 29
short ribs
    South-of-the-Border Short Ribs, 193
shrimp
    Roasted Shrimp with Romesco Dip, 116
Simple Green Salad, 129
Skillet Dressing, 147
Skillet Potatoes, 97
slow, slow, quick, quick cooking strategies, 186
Smashed Minty Peas, 98
smoothie
    Piña Colada Smoothie, 161

soup
    Black Bean Blender Soup, 172
    Mexican Pumpkin Soup, 173
South-of-the-Border Short Ribs, 193
South-of-the-Border Sundaes, 54
soy sauce
    gluten-free, 5
Spanish green olives, 8
Spanish Tortilla, 113
spatulas, 12
    silicone, 12
Spiced Basmati Rice with Cashews, 75
Spicy Noodles, 189
Spicy Pear Chutney, 190
Spicy Quick Pickles, 48
spinach, 6
    Egg Florentine Cups, 165
    frozen, 6
    Pistachio-Spinach Pesto, 171
    Spinach Salad with Mushrooms, Red Onions,
        and Cranberries, 81
spoons, cooking, 12
Spring Fling Supper, 94
Steakhouse Filet Mignon, 121
steaks
    testing the temperature of, 121
sticky rice, 87
stock
    gluten-free, 6
strainers, 12
strawberries, 119
    Balsamic Strawberries with Mascarpone
        Cream, 99
    Chocolate-Strawberry Fool, 124
    frozen, 6
sugar, 8–9
Sugar-Free Recipes
    Banana-Date Muffins, 164
    Breakfast Quesadilla, 162
    Egg Florentine Cups, 165
    Vegan Breakfast Bars, 166
    Whole Grain Overnight Porridge,
        163
sundaes
    Hot Cherry Sundaes, 71
    South-of-the-Border Sundaes, 54

sunflower butter, 8
suppers, 32–99
    Asian-Inspired Salmon and Rice Supper, 44
    Asian Ragu Supper, 83
    Cottage Comfort Supper, 77
    Curry in a Hurry Supper, 72
    Greek Burgers and Fries Supper, 55
    Quick Comfort Supper, 62
    Spring Fling Supper, 94
    See also dinners
sweeteners, 8–9
sweet potatoes
    Maple Mashed Sweet Potatoes, 149
    Roasted Sweet Potato Wedges, 128
sweet rice flour, 8
sweet rice flour blend
    preparing one's own, 17
    Sweet Rice Flour Blend, 8

tabasco, 5
tabbouleh
    Quinoa Tabbouleh, 92
taco sauce
    gluten-free, 5
tahini
    Creamy Tahini Sauce, 91
Tapas Party, 110
tapioca starch, 5, 9
tenderloin
    Pistachio-Cranberry-Goat Cheese–Stuffed
        Pork Tenderloin, 127
    Roasted Beef Tenderloin with Red Onion
        Gravy, 154
Thai Carrot and Cucumber Salad, 86
Thanksgiving Quick Dinner, 144
thyme, 5
Tinkyada brand, 5
tomatoes
    Baked Tomatoes, 65
    canned, 4
    Ricotta and Tomato Pasta, 41
    San Marzano tomatoes, 4
tomato sauce
    jarred, 7
tongs, 12
tortilla, Spanish, 113

Index

trifle
  Quick Black Forest Trifle, 158
tuna
  canned, 4
tzatziki
  Quick Tzatziki Sauce, 58

Vegan Breakfast Bars, 166
Vegenaise brand, 7
vegetables
  Bean and Veggie Chili, 178
  frozen, 6
  precut, 73
  preprepped, 12
  Vegetable Curry, 74
  washing, 11
Vegetarian/Vegan Adaptable Recipes
  Black Bean Blender Soup, 172
  Mexican Pumpkin Soup, 173
  Spicy Noodles, 189
  Whole Grain Biscuits, 28
Vegetarian/Vegan Recipes
  Bean and Veggie Chili, 178
  Pantry Salad, 176
  Pistachio-Spinach Pesto, 171
  prejudice against, 166
  Quick Roasted Beet Salad, 174
  Vegan Breakfast Bars, 166
vinegar, 9

washing fruits and vegetables, 11
Weeknight Mexican Fiesta, 49

whisks, 12
white beans
  Wine- and Rosemary-Braised Lamb Shanks
    with White Bean Mash, 195
white rice flour, 9
white wine vinegar, 9
whole grains
  Whole Grain Biscuits, 28
  Whole Grain Muffins and Quick Breads,
    26
  Whole Grain Overnight Porridge, 163
  Whole Grain Pancake and Biscuit Mix,
    24
  Whole Grain Pancakes, 25
  Whole Grain Quick Breads, 26
wine
  Sangaritas, 112
  Wine- and Rosemary-Braised Lamb Shanks
    with White Bean Mash, 195
Worcestershire sauce, 5

xanthan gum, 9

yogurt
  Creamy Tahini Sauce, 91
  Instant Berry Frozen Yogurt, 66
Yorkshire Puddings, Mini, 155

zest
  Mini Almond Orange Cakes, 117
  Roasted Corn with Chili-Lime Butter,
    141